cults
too good to be true

cults

too good to be true

RAPHAEL ARON

HarperCollins*Publishers*

HarperCollins*Publishers*

First published in Australia in 1999
by HarperCollins*Publishers* Pty Limited
ACN 009 913 517
A member of HarperCollins*Publishers* (Australia) Pty Limited Group
http://www.harpercollins.com.au

HarperCollins*Publishers*
25 Ryde Road, Pymble, Sydney, NSW 2073, Australia
31 View Road, Glenfield, Auckland 10, New Zealand
77–85 Fulham Palace Road, London W6 8JB, United Kingdom
Hazelton Lanes, 55 Avenue Road, Suite 2900, Toronto, Ontario M5R 3L2
and 1995 Markham Road, Scarborough, Ontario M1B 5M8, Canada
10 East 53rd Street, New York NY 10022, USA

National Library Cataloguing-in-Publication data:

Aron, Raphael
    Cults: too good to be true.
    ISBN 1 86371 760 9.
    1. Cults. 2. Cults - Australia. 3. Sects. 4. Sects -
    Australia. 5. Religions. 6. Counselling - Religious
    aspects. I. Title.
291

Cover photo: Mobs/International Photographic Library
Printed in Australia by Griffin Press Pty Ltd on 79gsm Bulky Paperback

5 4 3 2 1
03 02 01 00 99

CONTENTS

ACKNOWLEDGEMENTS   ix

INTRODUCTION   1

Part 1 UNDERSTANDING CULTS   7
1 – The Changing Cult Scene   10
2 – What is a Cult and Whom Does It Attract?   14
3 – The Difference Between a Cult and a Religion   24
4 – The Murder of Gilli Kroy   29
5 – The Entry Process   35

Part 2 WHAT DO THE CULTS BELIEVE?   39
6 – Cults and Belief Systems   41
7 – Fundamentalism and Exclusivity   47
8 – 'Suffer The Little Children'   52
9 – Lynette Phillips Burns Herself to Death   56
10 – The Power of Money   62
11 – Clairvoyants, Psychics and Fortune Tellers   65
12 – Satanic Cults   76
13 – The Apocalypse, Armageddon and the End-Times   80

Part 3 CULTS, CHILDREN AND THE MENTALLY ILL   85
14 – Cults and Children   87
15 – Cults and The Mentally Ill   97

Part 4 MIND CONTROL AND EXIT COUNSELLING   102
16 – But What is Mind Control?   104
17 – The Challenge of Exit Counselling   112
18 – Family Division Over Exit Counselling   117

Part 5 WHAT SHOULD WE DO NOW?   122
19 – We Are So Concerned – What Should We Do?   124
20 – Co-operation and Confidentiality   128
21 – What Are Our Choices?   133
22 – The Orientation Meeting   137

Part 6 THE INTERVENTION – Coming Home   146
23 – Debbie and the Mystic from Poona   148
24 – Michael and The Assembly of Light and Truth
     – A Mother Tells   166
25 – Exit Counselling – Reversing Mind Control   179

Part 7 WELCOME BACK TO THE REAL WORLD   185
26 – After the Intervention – The Beginning of a New Journey   188
27 – Feelings and Fears – Living With Oneself   193
28 – Integration – Relating to the Community   199
29 – Marriage, Personal Relationships, Dating and Sex   203
30 – What About the Children?   208
31 – After the Cult – The Family   212

Part 8 EXIT COUNSELLING IS NOT ALWAYS THE ANSWER   216
32 – But We Can't Do It!   218
33 – What To Do If the Exit Counselling Doesn't Work   222
34 – Other Reasons Not To Go Ahead   227
35 – Governments and Lawmakers Can No Longer Sit Still   231

EPILOGUE   236

ENDNOTES   239

BIBLIOGRAPHY   249

Dedicated to my wife, Shani and our children,
Levi and Robin, Devorah Leah and Yankie,
Brocho, Rachmi, Menucha, Chaya, Kivi, Yosef and Menachem

ACKNOWLEDGEMENTS

First and foremost I would like to thank my wife, Shani who has supported my involvement in this complex field of work and encouraged me to take on the task of writing this book. It is not possible to express true appreciation for Shani's patience and her willingness to accommodate the frequent travel, the after hours calls and the day-to-day pressures of this often very unorthodox work.

To my children who are only too familiar with packed suitcases and telephone calls from airports far and wide. My hope is that the impact on our family life will be outweighed by their increased awareness of the preciousness of each individual's life.

To my mother, Toni whose love of books has inspired me to put pen to paper and write this book. To the memory of my late father, Zek Akiva who taught me how to read and appreciate the written word.

To Ursula Rembach, my administrative assistant, for her untiring efforts in assisting with the extensive research required for this book. To Esther Spivak, my secretary, for her assistance in typing the manuscript.

To Joanna, Sarah, Michael and his parents, Ron and Anne for their willingness to be included in this book. To Ron for his candid account of life in a cult. Without these contributions, this book would not be able to broadcast its message to the community.

To the police for their assistance in responding to cult-related enquiries. To the media for their interest in this field of work and their cooperation in researching the cult arena.

To the authors and publishers in Australia and overseas who have granted permission for me to quote for their works in the writing of this book. A particular thankyou to Sarah Hamilton-Byrne in Australia and Wendy Ford in the USA for their permission to quote from their books.

To my agent Tim Curnow of Curtis Brown (Australia) and publisher, Cathy Jenkins of HarperCollins*Publishers* whose encouragement and invaluable advice assisted in bringing the original manuscript to publication standard. To Susannah Burgess of HarperCollins*Publishers* and Catherine Hammond of Catherine Hammond Editing Services for their assistance in the preparation and publication of this book.

To the numerous clients who have sought and continue to seek assistance through Cult Counselling Australia. Their strength and determination are an inspiration for so many individuals and families who are frightened and overwhelmed by the intensity and complexity of the cult problem.

I am reminded of the famous Rabbinic saying, 'It is not incumbent on you to complete the work; yet you are not free to desist from it.'

Raphael Aron

INTRODUCTION

'Some human beings seem to be driven by an overwhelming urge to espouse a cause and, failing to find one, may become fixated on astonishingly inferior substitutes. The instinctive need to be a member of a closely linked group fighting for common ideals may be so strong that it becomes inessential what these ideals are and whether they possess any intrinsic value.'[1]

Although the cult phenomenon is no longer something new, the pain inflicted by these organisations and the frustration incurred in trying to curtail their activities remain very real. Families, friends, community and religious leaders continue to seek adequate responses to a growing number of cult organisations and fringe churches. As the number of groups and their membership grow, the search continues to halt this disturbing trend and to provide assistance to those individuals who have been caught in its clutches.

Against this climate, parents and friends question whether their loved ones are involved in spiritual experimentation, which, like any other form of experimentation, be it drug use or sexual behaviour, needs to be tolerated. Yet they cannot help but wonder if there is something more sinister and potentially dangerous about these groups, which seem to be spreading across the world.

In 1993, the world was shocked as the Waco tragedy unfolded, with the eventual death of 83 men, women and children at the headquarters in Texas. In 1994, 53 members of the Order of the Solar temple died in what appeared to be a mass suicide, which took place simultaneously in Switzerland and Quebec. Later that year, in December, a further 16 people, including three children, were found in the charred remains of a remote Alpine village. In 1995, the infamous Japanese Aum Shinri Kyo cult was held responsible for the poisoning of 12 commuters, when nerve gas was released into the Japanese subway system. In 1997, the world was shocked by the suicide of 39 members of the Heaven's Gate cult, who left the earth in order to join the extra-terrestrial world of the comet Hale-Bopp.

This book documents cases which show that here in Australia, too, the cults have been responsible for death and suicide. Children have been separated from their families, and drugs have been administered to helpless patients without consent. Families have been torn apart as a result of the invasive and destructive agendas of cult organisations. Quiet countryside retreats have shielded numerous groups originating in the USA and Europe that have regarded Australia as a haven and a setting in which to establish themselves and attract new recruits and members whilst amassing fortunes. There is limited accountability and no code of ethics to govern many of these organisations. In effect, they are a law unto themselves.

In Australia in the past ten years we have seen the mushrooming of new self-development courses. Claiming to offer inner happiness, better business acumen and improved social skills, some of these groups appear to operate recklessly, in a manner which clearly exploits the members or participants. Although, on the surface, such groups may follow the direction of bona fide self-development organisations, a closer examination of their methods reveals a very different picture. Most of them are able to operate without controls or government scrutiny. The media has exposed some of these practices, but in other situations the only recourse for disenchanted families has been the court system. Marriages have been threatened, children have been neglected and the community has paid the price.

And to suggest that the casualties of the cult phenomenon are limited to those who die is to ignore the thousands upon thousands of families who have been ripped apart as a result of the influence of these groups. Young people who have gone missing, marriages and relationships which have broken up, families that are no longer together, and individuals who have lost their purpose in life — these are the living sacrifices of so many of these organisations.

Do parents and others have the right to intervene, to attempt to influence the direction which has been the 'choice' of the individual concerned? Is this not a breach of the inalienable right of freedom of choice and freedom of religion? What choices do parents have when a loved one departs from home for no reason and no intention to return? To whom do the parents turn in their time of crisis?

This book attempts to address these issues. It has been written in order to give the reader an opportunity to understand the cult phenomenon. I aim to show that cults are not a black and white issue and that the attention they have received publicly and through the media is often inaccurate, unjust and misleading.

In particular, I attempt to discuss the defining characteristics of a cult and the notion of destructive cultism. Cults *are* destructive because of the level of control they wield over their following. Whereas most social systems and families involve various degrees of control and subservience to authority, cults cross a critical line, creating an unnatural community which ultimately involves the loss of members' freedom and independence.

In writing the book, I draw from my experience and work with hundreds of cases, both in Australia and overseas, in order to present individuals, families and concerned citizens with a framework and structure through which they can resolve issues which may rank amongst the most difficult they have had to deal with during their entire lives — the future and destiny of a son or a daughter, a husband or a wife, a loved one or a friend.

Although some of the material is drawn form well-publicised cases, I have used pseudonyms where appropriate to protect the identity of the people involved. In some situations, former members and their families may have agreed to their stories being published some years ago. However, it may no longer be in their interests for attention to be drawn to these experiences.

When I commenced working in the field twenty years ago, books such as *Snapping: America's Epidemic of Sudden Personality Change*[2] broke new ground in introducing the world to the concepts of psychological manipulation, mind control and personality change. At the time, I sensed a level of scepticism regarding this analysis.

Since then, the body of information has grown, professional organisations have grown up, and eminent professionals have endorsed the works of others who have studied the cult phenomenon and its widespread ramifications. Journals, periodicals and a range of books, from both a professional and a lay perspective, have become available. The establishment of standards and criteria by which groups can be managed has lent further credibility to the way in which cultism is being approached.

This is important for two reasons. Firstly, for the reader to appreciate that cultism *is* a unique issue, which deserves a special understanding as well as treatment. It shouldn't and can't be looked upon as just another fad, which eventually will go away. It isn't a fad and it won't go away.

Secondly, to inform the reader that the results of research have facilitated the availability of numerous resources which provide information and guidelines to exit counsellors, therapists and other professionals. Although this book has drawn from some of these resources, my intention has been to present cultism in lay terms for the broader community. Families and professionals should, nevertheless, be aware of the wealth of material which now exists and, where necessary, utilise these resources.

The increase in cult activity and the failure of the relevant authorities to take a more pro-active stand are reasons for concern. Against this backdrop there are, nevertheless, numerous lessons to be learnt and generous opportunities for families to be optimistic. This book is designed to examine the options and help create the opportunities.

Ultimately, the purpose of this book is to provide the reader with inner strength and renewed hope.

Raphael Aron

PART 1

UNDERSTANDING CULTS

- THE CHANGING CULT SCENE

- WHAT IS A CULT AND WHOM DOES IT ATTRACT?

- THE DIFFERENCE BETWEEN A CULT AND A RELIGION

- THE MURDER OF GILLI KROY

- THE ENTRY PROCESS

During the mid-1970s, I was a student at Melbourne University. My interest in counselling took me to the chaplaincy, where I would spend a few hours a week speaking to the counsellors and, where possible, sitting in on a number of sessions.

It was during the final examination period in 1974 when I received a phone call from a distraught mother who claimed that her daughter had become involved in a cult. She wanted to know what to do and whom to talk to. Unsure about how to handle it, I organised an appointment, hoping that in the meantime I could research this intriguing problem. My research efforts were fruitless and frustrating. There was hardly a person I could speak with who knew anything about cults. Several people suggested I try to establish contact with American counselling agencies, but I wasn't sure where to start. Others suggested I speak directly with the group which was allegedly 'hiding' this girl.

A week later a second call came through. This time it was about a woman who had left her husband and two young children to travel to India to see a guru. She had left no contact address or phone number, and her husband and brother were very concerned.

It would be an understatement to say that these two phone calls changed my life and, I believe, the lives of many people I have worked with since. As a believer in the concept of Divine Providence, I was not able to ignore these calls and decided to look further into this seemingly very powerful phenomenon of cultism — something so powerful that it appeared to be able to split families and destroy relationships.

The journey which started in 1974 is still continuing. Every year I work with hundreds of individuals, both in Australia and overseas, who have become involved in cults.

The first step on that journey was the opportunity for me to witness and experience the cults first-hand. I managed to do this by visiting numerous different groups and participating in their activities. I studied Transcendental Meditation, attended the Hare Krishna temple, was audited by Scientology and meditated at Siddha Yoga. Later on I attended an est training session and went fundraising with the Moonies.

I attended conferences in the United States and subscribed to numerous magazines, journals and press-clipping services. The more I researched the phenomenon of cultism, the more my eyes were opened to the complex and intricate nature of these groups, which were labelled destructive. It became clear that the public, the media and the clergy had underestimated the nature and extent of the cult issue; cults were a very specific psychological phenomenon and called for special attention.

The Jonestown tragedy in 1978 was a significant turning point in awakening the world to the danger of destructive groups.

For me personally it represented a compelling reason to establish a formal organisation to address this problem and deal with it. And thus The Jewish Centre was born. As a tiny organisation staffed by volunteers, the organisation was established to research cultism and assist families who were affected. Although initially funded by the Jewish community, the organisation catered for the broader community, providing information and resources as well as counselling and support to families concerned about the fate of their loved ones.

Today, Cult Counselling Australia has replaced The Jewish Centre and, as a community-based non-profit organisation, continues to offer a wide range of services to families throughout Australia and overseas.

It is well over twenty years since I commenced this work. Nevertheless, despite significant changes in the presentation of the numerous cults in Australia and around the world, the fundamental issue remains the same: the psychological and emotional harm inflicted on the unsuspecting individuals who join these groups and the resulting damage to families and the broader community.

Over the years, I have witnessed the pain of families being torn apart, the trauma of not knowing the whereabouts of a loved one and the grief arising out of a cult-related suicide. But I have also been part of family reunion and reconciliation, the re-establishment of relationships and the restoration of individual freedom.

These positive outcomes have provided the inspiration to continue an important task which commenced as a result of two phone calls over twenty years ago.

CHAPTER 1

THE CHANGING CULT SCENE

'Cults are so sophisticated today', says Inger Messina, the mother of a member of the Church Universal and Triumphant. 'It's not like it used to be with the Moonies on street corners with flowers. They now like pin-striped business suits. Cults are big organizations.' [1]

An assessment of the cult scene in the 1970s reveals the growth of a number of large organisations, with headquarters in India or the USA. Popular names associated with the cult scene included Hare Krishna, Rajneesh (also known as the Orange People), Divine Light Mission, The Children of God, the Moonies and Transcendental Meditation.

Other individuals and groups had also drawn attention around the world. The Ananda Marga movement had attracted attention due to a well-publicised suicide by one of its Australian members on the doorstep of the United Nations in 1978.

Patty Hearst and the Symbionese Liberation Army, Charles Manson and the Tate LaBianca murders and the suicide of 914 people at Jonestown in Guyana highlighted the seriousness of the cult issue and also galvanised popular opinion against these organisations.

Today the situation is radically different and far less defined, with the emergence of new groups, many of which have received no publicity and about which very little, if anything, is known. Throughout the world, the list of organisations which draw attention continues to grow. These groups vary in size from single digit numbers to large organisations claiming membership in the hundreds and thousands. They have a diverse range of agendas.

Although most of these groups will be referred to later, a sampling includes Siddha Yoga, Sahaja Yoga, Rajneesh, Divine Light Mission, Ananda Marga, Sai Baba, The Children of God, The Love Family, The Way International, The Exclusive Brethren, E-Min, The Church of Scientology, Jehovah's Witnesses, The Centre of Knowledge and Supremacy, The Unification Church (the Moonies), The Church Universal and Triumphant, Anne Hamilton-Byrne, est and Money and You.

A disturbing development is the emergence of personal development courses run by organisations or individuals with hidden, often corrupt, agendas. Because these organisations do not wear the 'religious' mantle, they are often unwittingly ignored in an assessment of the overall cult scene. Yet their practices are often no different from those of the better-known cults.

In an article 'Cults Not Gone, Just Mainstreaming',[2] Marcia Rudin, Director of the International Cult Program of the American Family Foundation, refers to the wide variety of cults that attract followers by offering mind-empowerment, psychotherapy, business opportunities and political activism. Rather than promising spiritual salvation or ultimate meaning, they skilfully market themselves to a new clientele by offering financial success, happiness, social success and self-fulfilment. These groups do not appeal to the young 'counterculture' seekers of the 1960s and 1970s but to older, affluent, established, 'normal' people.

Cults do not require a large organisational structure headed by a well-known guru. The same dynamics that exist within that setting can be replicated in considerably smaller groups with dire consequences. The situation in which a particular person has taken control of another person's life is no different and is sometimes even more dangerous.

The exploitative and opportunistic use of alternative medicine by untrained practitioners is also cause for concern. Quite apart from the damage done to the reputation of the genuine workers in these fields, these charlatans have selfishly and often dangerously used their positions to harm well-meaning and unsuspecting clients. Documented cases of split families and broken marriages resulting from these practices are a direct result of the lack of control and standards in this growing industry.

Concerns have been raised regarding the cult-like techniques used by multi-level marketing organisations, such as Amway, to attract recruits and maintain their allegiance. Some multi-level marketing organisations appear to adopt an almost evangelical and cult-like approach, suggesting that involvement in their marketing programs will affect the participants' quality of life and sense of purpose. Other issues of concern include the creation of a sense of dependence on the organisation, as well as the discouragement of creativity and individuality.

The phenomenon of channelling[3] is becoming increasingly popular. The idea that a physical, embodied human being can communicate information from an outer source and different dimension of reality has attracted considerable interest. As the messages of entities like 'Lazaris', 'Ramtha' and 'Seth' are channelled down to earth, there is concern about the impact of this phenomenon and the similarity of related behaviour to some of the cults.

Many of the older cults have re-established themselves by decentralising, operating out of smaller settings in the broader community, which makes them less vulnerable to scrutiny. The use of the Internet allows cults to broadcast their message on a global scale. Young people, teenagers and adolescents can connect with cults at the press of a button.

A home page called *The David Koresh Research Centre*, dedicated to the Branch Davidian Waco siege of 1993, is one of the largest cult websites. While not directly supporting the teachings of Koresh, it offers Internet surfers copies of his letters, quotes and Bible study transcripts.

Dr Michael Carr-Gregg, from the Centre of Adolescent Health in Melbourne, writes, 'Of course, our children don't need to leave home to be seduced; the Internet is replete with a variety of spiritual predators, using chat sites to spread their gospel and glossy graphics to lure new members.'[4]

Clearly, advances in the field of information technology have assisted the smaller, less financial groups in advancing their causes. Whereas, twenty years ago, the cults required a structure and some form of corporate identity in order to spread their word and promote their cause, today, with little more than a modem and a PC, a small group or single operator can access the world market. There is every reason to believe that this trend will continue.

CHAPTER 2

WHAT IS A CULT AND WHOM DOES IT ATTRACT?

'She lived in, and created for us, a world of deceptions, lies and inconsistencies ... By her control over the spiritual aspects of our lives, by her subjugation of us by physical means, and by her constant assault on our belief in our own worth, Anne was able to systematically break down our sense of self.

'The bulk of the cult was made up of professional people. Without their support and participation, Anne Hamilton-Byrne would not have become what she is today ... These professional people — doctors, lawyers, engineers, architects, psychiatrists, nurses and social workers — allowed her successfully to pull the wool over everyone's eyes for more than twenty years.

'It is very difficult to understand why the core members, those who knew most about Anne, adhered to her bizarre beliefs. In comparison with her, many must have been of superior intellect and almost all were better educated ... Surely, some of these people should have been clever enough to look beyond the veneer of spirituality and see the hypocrisy of preaching asceticism while living in self-indulgent luxury?' [1]

Most people who call me are keen to find out whether a particular organisation or group is a 'cult'. Often, the information they present is very vague or coloured by the particular experience of the person who has become involved. The difficulty is that the term 'cult' appears to have been applied to so many situations that it is easy to see why people have difficulty in finding an appropriate 'user-friendly' definition.

In the introduction to *Recovery from Cults*,[2] Michael Langone defines a cult as follows:

> A cult is a group or movement that, to a significant degree, (a) exhibits great or excessive devotion or dedication to some idea or thing, (b) uses a thought reform program to persuade, control and socialize members (i.e to integrate them into the group's unique pattern of relationships, beliefs, values and practices), (c) systematically induces states of psychological dependency in members, (d) exploits members to advance the leadership's goals, and (e) causes psychological harm to members, their families and the community.

According to Robert J. Lifton, Professor of Psychology and Psychiatry at John Jay College and the Graduate Center of the City University of New York, cults can be identified by three characteristics: (a) a charismatic leader who increasingly becomes an object of worship as the general principles which may have sustained the group lose power; (b) a process of coercive persuasion or thought reform; (3) economic, sexual and other exploitation of group members by the leader.[3]

EIGHT CHARACTERISTICS OF A CULT

One of the best-known sets of criteria by which a cult can be judged has also been provided by Robert Lifton.[4] Lifton has studied Chinese thought reform of the 1950s as well as the psychology of Nazi doctors. In doing so he has arrived at a list of eight definitive characteristics of cult organisations. These eight characteristics have since become a mental health standard. He suggests that the best way to determine whether a particular group is destructive is to compare its behaviour and conduct with these eight criteria.

1   **Milieu Control** refers to total control of communication in the group; for example, no gossip or expression of doubt about the group. Members have to report peers who break any rules, have limited or no contact with relatives and ignore anything in the media.

  Members of the Exclusive Brethren are restricted from using television, radios, computers, record and CD players. A leader of the group in New Zealand, Malcolm Edward says "We don't like using the airwaves normally. Satan is the prince of the power of the air and that medium is used to get right into a believer's home. We don't want that.[5]

2   **Loading of the Language** is the imposition of a language which is unique to the cult. The continued use of particular clichés and expressions creates a sense of camaraderie, which unites the members and sets them apart from the world, which, in some groups, is described as satanic, evil or unclean.

  In Re-Evaluation Counselling, a group which has come under attack in the US for its cult-like methods, words such as yawning, counselling or discharge are given new meanings; the outside world does not use the words of phrases in the same way. Former members agree that the use of these expressions and many others keeps them united and focused on the techniques and processes of the group.[6]

3   **A Demand for Purity** refers to a radical separation of good and bad. The cult is right, the world is wrong. Acts are either good or bad, and people are viewed in black-and-white terms. Purity allows the cult to let the ends justify the

means; deception and lying are acceptable if they serve the pure aim of the cult.

Most apocalyptic cults spread the message that you are either a member of the group — and will survive, or you are not — and won't survive. In order to save people and draw them into the group, you can lie, because those who are saved will ultimately appreciate your action.

In 1987, The Centre of Knowledge and Supremacy was a small cult operating in Queensland and Victoria. One of its publications included the following introduction: 'For the true seekers, may this book be the eternal beacon of Light they have sought which will lead them to their true abode. For those evil beings of Darkness, may it be the eternal flame which will reduce their bodies, minds and souls to ashes.'[7]

4 **Confession** refers to the process by which members admit everything about their past and present behaviour. Although the member is told that the confession will set him free, in effect it binds him to the group. Later on, the information can be used against him. Leaving the cult becomes more difficult, as the member feels that he will have left behind an intimate part of himself.

   Some personal development groups, such as Money and You, an organisation operating in Australia, involve activities in which you share your innermost feelings with other participants. Such sharing reinforces powerful allegiance to the group.

5 **Mystical manipulation** — or planned spontaneity — refers to a process whereby the members feel they have chosen to belong to the group; a belief is created that allegiance to the cult is a totally voluntary act. Events in the cult are planned to look spontaneous, when, in fact, they are carefully orchestrated by the leadership.

   According to Erica Heftman, a former member of the Moonies and author of the book Behind the Darker Side of the Moonies, 'there were jokes we told every day, there were stories which were made to sound spontaneous, but everything was planned beforehand'.[8]

6   **Doctrine Over Person** requires the member to interpret reality through the cult doctrine and to ignore personal experiences or reality. If the member's experience is at odds with the cult dogma, the experience is disregarded. Contradictions become associated with guilt; doubt indicates one's own deficiency or evil.

   Bhagwan Rajneesh, the former guru of a group known as the Orange People wrote in his newsletter, 'The Master first has to destroy all your beliefs theist, atheist, Catholic, communist — the Master has to dismantle all your structures of belief, so that you are left again as a small child, innocent, open, ready to inquire, ready to plunge into the adventures of truth.'[9]

7   **Sacred Science** refers to the leader's claim to wisdom and the fact that his philosophy and belief system are relevant to all humankind. Anyone who disagrees is not only immoral but unscientific.

   American-born Franklin Jones, now known by his devotees as Adi Da, the Da Avatar, writes, "I am the inherent being. I am the perfectly subjective truth of the world, made incarnate, plain, and obvious as man, and to man. I am the life and consciousness of all beings.[10]

8   **Dispensing of Existence** means that those who have not seen the light are wedded to evil, tainted and lack the right to exist. Hence, a cult member threatened with being cast into outer darkness may experience a fear of extinction or collapse. This is the final step in creating members' dependence on the group.

   A former member of the Moonies in Melbourne sought counselling with me over a fear that because she had left the group she would not become pregnant. It took several years before she overcame the fear.

Many people think that cult involvement will invariably mean donning a sari, a name change (usually to an Indian Sanskrit alternative), the loss of study or employment opportunities, a major financial commitment and a possible total breakdown in family communication. Whilst some of this may be true, it is rare that a cult will call for every one of these practices.

Many cults have no visible Eastern connections, and there is no outward indication whatsoever of affiliation. Some family communication may be maintained and the cult member may remain in employment. What does lie at the heart of the cult experience, however, is the process of psychological manipulation, whereby the individual loses freedom and the ability to make independent decisions. The cult victim becomes totally dependent on the cult's system, authority and environment and essentially substitutes this newfound orientation for their family of origin and earlier belief system.

Not all cults are 'religious' in nature. Many cults use religion and spirituality in order to achieve their goals; however, there are many other types of cults. Some pyramid selling organisations, psychotherapeutic and personal development groups and even some individual therapists can create situations which are no less cult-like than those created by certain swamis and gurus in ashrams and temples. If anything, because some of these groups do not present as religious or spiritual in nature, the innocent participant is at even greater risk of being duped and eventually controlled.

In the final analysis, the real danger of the cult is the power and control which is vested in the leader and the image of omnipotence which he/she assumes. In turn, their mind-manipulated followers continue to surrender their independence and decision-making abilities, including their most precious possessions: their children, partners, privacy, money and, ultimately, their minds.

Who is vulnerable?

The cult phenomenon cuts across all borders, be they racial, social, religious or economic. Vulnerability to the effects of destructive cults is often unrecognised until it is too late. Mental ability, a high IQ, social integration, success and ambition have not prevented cults from taking their toll on the very members of the community who would seem least vulnerable to their influences.

The leader of The Centre of Knowledge and Supremacy was a doctor. His right-hand man was a lecturer in philosophy at La Trobe University in Melbourne.

Although everyone is vulnerable to the influences of cults, there appear to be particular situations which lend themselves to cult involvement. Low points, at which time life becomes more difficult, illness, death of a loved one and times of crisis or soul-searching — all these create opportunities for cult groups to offer assistance in the form of counselling, accommodation and even shelter. An unhappy relationship, conflict at home, communication problems, unemployment and financial difficulty can also create a sense of vulnerability. Failure, a loss of self-esteem and a sense of hopelessness further weaken resistance to outside influences, whether positive or counter-productive.

Times of spiritual turmoil, feelings of rejection by one's chosen church and a need to find a deeper meaning in life can also direct the searching individual to other alternatives, whose attraction is magnified as a result of these circumstances. Family situations which have never been resolved and conflicts regarding identity can help create the climate in which the helping hand of the cult is welcome.

Although the above situations may set the scene for cult involvement, it is wrong to assume that stable relationships, steady employment and a high self-esteem will guarantee insulation from the cult experience. They do provide a healthier anchor, however, with strong ties which, in turn, will serve as some counterbalance to the opportunities offered by the cult.

Some contact with various groups and organisations is inevitable; not every contact with a cult group or a connection with some of its members is reason for alarm. An inappropriate or overreaction to such contact can be as counter-productive as a failure to address a potentially dangerous situation. It is foolish to assume that every encounter with a New Age group, a suspected cult or a personal development organisation will end with suicide or murder! These irrational thoughts serve only to create panic and anxiety and lead to inappropriate responses to the young seeker who wants guidance and not condemnation.

Although experimentation carries risks, as the community has seen in relation to drug abuse and sexual permissiveness, it is a fact of life that people will try out new experiences. The level of reaction due in response to this experimentation will depend on the particular situation and circumstances.

The key to ensuring that the initial brush or contact with a cult does not develop into full-blown involvement lies in early detection. If parents can be knowledgeable and alert, there is a greater chance that they will be able to assist their loved ones in assessing whether a group is destructive or not.

GOOD QUESTIONS TO ASK

There are numerous questions which parents and individuals can use to help them assess whether a group is a cult. They include the following:

- What is so appealing about what the group offers?
- Does the leader have special charm and powers of persuasion that the group's members find hard to resist?
- Do the people in the group seem too friendly, loving, smiling or happy?

- Does the group claim to have a special mission or unique calling?
- Does the leader claim to have unique powers, vision, knowledge or other abilities?
- Do the people talk about their leader as if the person were next to God?
- What are the background and credentials of the leader?
- Does the group motivate its members through fear or guilt?
- Have any articles been written about the group? Any books?
- Are there any disgruntled former members?
- Who invited you to the group? Was it a total stranger?[11]

Although many of these questions will be relevant to all cults, there are a number of issues which should be canvassed in relation to personal development groups. They include the following:

- Does the group promise happiness, total fulfilment, greater self-confidence and a solution to all your problems? If so, beware — it's too good to be true.
- Are you offered testimonials of former participants still enthusiastic about their experience, instead of hard facts? Are you expected to blindly follow people you don't know?
- Does the group give you a concise view of all the courses offered? If not, you may find yourself moving endlessly from one course to the next.
- Be wary of courses which are designed for *everyone* and beneficial to all.
- Is there pressure to sign up quickly?

- Are methods used by the group which weaken your sense of reality, such as long hours, little sleep or deprivation of food?
- Does the group offer a written contract and cancellation form, as well as a statement detailing the number of hours, all the costs and the terms of payment?

Don't be afraid to call a professional cult agency in order to discuss your concerns. These organisations have been established to assist you. Just one phone call may avert a frightening nightmare.

CHAPTER 3

THE DIFFERENCE BETWEEN
A CULT AND A RELIGION

'On March 20, 1986, Janet Cole drove from Seattle to Portland and drowned her five-year-old daughter Brittany, in a motel bathtub. The attractive thirty-seven-year-old mother, described by friends as the ideal Christian woman, was convinced that she was demon-possessed and that a similar fate would probably befall her daughter. She wanted the little girl to go to heaven and so committed an act of love by killing her. Janet Cole was a member of a large Pentecostal church, Community Chapel, in South Seattle that ex-members and other critics claim was preoccupied with demons and "deliverance ministry".'[1]

In 1980, WCCO-TV in Minneapolis, Minnesota, produced a documentary entitled *Thy Will Be Done*. Although some of the material is now dated, this production ranks amongst the best documentaries produced on the cult problem. In the documentary, Professor Margaret Singer sets out the differences between a cult and a religion.

Professor Singer states that within a monastic order even the lowliest monks have access to higher levels and can seek justice outside the order. Not so with the cults, where the hierarchal structure denies any contact between the members/followers and the higher echelons of power. Cults have a double set of ethics: within the group you must be open and honest and confess all to the leader; however, outside the group you can deceive and manipulate. In contrast, established religions and ethical groups teach members to be honest and truthful and abide by one set of ethics.[2]

Perhaps the most significant difference between a cult and a religion is the fact that in the latter the veneration is directed towards God, whereas in a cult the love and devotion is directed towards itself. The leader is either God-manifest or God himself. There is no room for question or doubt. Allied with this notion is the belief in the leader's infallibility. This belief has far-reaching implications.

Total and unquestioning commitment to a guru or a master carries the risk that in the event the leader becomes paranoid or deranged, the followers will have no choice but to remain loyal to the whims of his madness. The tragedies of Jonestown, Waco and Heaven's Gate involved leaders who, at one time, had credibility. Jim Jones, for example, commenced his work as an ordained member of a Christian Church and was highly regarded by various US dignitaries.

The notion of infallibility leads many cult members to believe that life without the cult leader is unthinkable. In the event of the leader's death, the cult members may choose one of two options: to believe that the leader has not really died, as was the case of Bhagwan Shree Rajneesh, guru of the Rajneesh organisation, whose death was viewed as the shedding of a physical cloak; or tragically to follow their leader by committing suicide.

There are other differences between cults and religions. Religious groups support the family structure and can be credited with attempting to emphasise its importance in the face of the collapse of the nuclear family. They encourage family contact as well as the use of counselling services to heal relationships. Religious leaders do not assume the role of parents.

Religious orders will not disguise information about the true nature of the organisation, its beliefs and its structure. There are opportunities to question and to inquire. In the mainstream churches, the mission statements, the methods of appointments and the financial records are available to the public. All of these issues are an 'open book'. Cults, on the other hand, make a deliberate effort to conceal the true nature of the group by operating under a variety of names or withholding information from the potential recruit.

The restriction on inquiry or criticism of the organisation is a very disturbing feature of many cults. In his book, *When God Becomes a Drug: Breaking the Chains of Religious Addiction and Abuse*, L. Booth suggests that the discouragement of independent thinking is the primary identifying mark of a dysfunctional system. 'If you cannot question or examine what you are taught, if you cannot doubt or challenge authority, you are in danger of being victimised or abused.'[3]

Religions do not divide the world between the good — those who follow the religion — and the bad — those who do not follow it. This division of the world into good and evil is one of the features of cults which is almost universal. Whether the message is presented overtly or subtly, the followers are led to believe that their way is the only way; any departure from the cult and its beliefs is fraught with danger.

The tendency to divide the world into good and evil is also a characteristic of the 'fringe churches', which are becoming increasingly popular today. These churches, which present as bona fide Christian organisations, are often guilty of the misrepresentation and deceit practised by some of the better-known cults. (The fringe churches are covered in greater detail in a later chapter.)

The complaint against the cult is not the fact that it is secretive; it is the fact that the group is deceitful, making every effort to conceal its true aims, the potential effect on the follower and family — not to speak of the implication of the group's ideology on relationships, friendships, employment, study and social interaction.

In contrast, fraternities such as the Masons, which are secretive, openly inform members that they will be taught the more secret rituals of the group as they progress. As Professor Singer says very succinctly, 'A secret handshake is not equivalent to mind control.'[4]

In order to show how cults differ from religions, Dr Flavil Yeakley, from the Abilene Christian University, administered a personality profile research device to hundreds of members of religious groups, both from the established religions and the cults.

In the cult context, he administered the tests to members of the Boston Church of Christ, the Church of Scientology, the Hare Krishnas, Maranatha, the Children of God, the Moonies and the Way International. The same test was given to members of the Baptist, Catholic, Lutheran, Methodist and Presbyterian churches and 'mainline' Churches of Christ.

The results showed that people in certain cults appeared to be all moving toward the same type of personalities regardless of the original personalities they brought with them into the group. By contrast, in the established churches, there was no indication of conformity to any type of personality. People's fundamental personality types remained intact.[5]

As clear as the line between religions and cults may be, the situation changes as we slide into the abyss of religious fundamentalism. Graphic images of suicide bombers in Israel or Pakistan and terrorism in the name of religion raise disturbing questions. These types of activity suggest that within a particular setting and under the right conditions, the same issues of mind control and psychological manipulation can creep into the religious domain, presenting a picture no less dangerous or horrifying than the cult experience itself. The same processes are at work, even though there may not be the organisational structure which is representative of cultism.

We should also draw a line between the so-called mind control techniques which are used by numerous destructive cults and the conditioning process which we are all exposed to as part of growing up in our own environment. By their very nature, the environment we live in, the people around us and our own families influence and shape our thinking, attitudes and values. It is a natural process, which creates change as we develop and mature — not a contrived or controlling process, the beneficiary of which is an outsider or an organisation. The tragic irony is that despite the fact that the cults' practices are deceitful and destructive, their very nature has enabled them to reach out and attract hundreds of thousands of followers, many of whom have renounced their earlier religious affiliations.

It's a cruel reality that the religions which preach tolerance and love have been supplanted by organisations that speak of hatred and division. Such is the challenge that faces the established religions today.

CHAPTER 4

THE MURDER OF GILLI KROY
— A Personal Story

'Don't let your mother get the better of you ever. Always maintain the view that you are in the right. Don't think about your mother's reproaches and don't bother yourself about whether she is justified or not. She is the impostor. She is very good at playing the pity game. Fake emotions. Call her once. Upset her and almost immediately hang up. Show how horrible she is.'[1]

The story of Gilli Kroy provides a graphic and tragic example of the potential danger of cults: in particular, when family conflict is involved. The case centred around a desperate mother's efforts to rescue her daughter, Talli, from the clutches of a cult which had already gained the allegiance and following of her husband, Moishe.

The cult, a little-known group operating under the name of the Church of Knowledge and Supremacy, had centres in Queensland and Victoria on mainland Australia.

Gilli's story goes back to the time the family was living in California. In mid-1986 they became involved with the group calling itself the Centre for Knowledge and Supremacy. The Centre's leader, Dr Joseph Chiappalone, a former Melbourne medical practitioner, was on tour in the United States, lecturing on his brand of metaphysics, which predicted an end to the world in fifteen years. He forecast that the end would start by large areas of Italy and Japan falling into the sea in August or September of that year.

Dr Chiappalone and his second wife, Amitakh Ng, a Malaysian-born spiritual medium, stayed with the Kroy family in San Francisco. It was there that the two men, Moishe Kroy and Joseph Chiappalone, who had known each other for years, discovered they were soul mates. Gilli discovered the reverse; she took an almost instant dislike to Dr Chiappalone.

Shortly after the Chiappalone visit, Dr Kroy returned to Australia with his daughter, Talli. They travelled via India, where they visited the ashram of the guru Sai Baba. Some months later Gilli returned to Melbourne to find that her marriage had broken up and that Talli had no desire to have any relationship with her.

Two lengthy Family Court battles followed. Gilli was denied access to her daughter on the grounds that Talli was old enough to decide for herself and she had chosen her father.

At the time, I was unsuccessful in my attempts to convince the Family Court of the unique nature of this case and the distinct possibility that Talli was a victim of mind control. In an affidavit submitted to the Family Court of Australia at Melbourne on the 5 May 1987, the deponent, Mr K.G. Bonsall of the firm Plotkins, Barristers and Solicitors, said *inter alia* that he was concerned about the matter in general and the child's welfare in particular. Mr Bonsall referred to my extreme concern regarding Talli Kroy's welfare and recommended that a separate representative be appointed to look after her welfare. He further recommended that I contribute to a report on the case as a matter of urgency.

That report was never prepared. Instead, I received a lengthy letter from Dr Kroy explaining how wrong I was and that my views of The Centre for Knowledge and Supremacy were misguided and false.

Gilli had been reduced to rummaging through her husband's garbage to try to find out what was happening to her daughter. Because of her desperate behaviour the Family Court eventually imposed restraining orders, which forbade her from contacting Talli or her husband. In September 1987, Talli's dislike of her mother had grown so intense that she told a television interviewer she hated her mother. Meanwhile Gilli also turned to the media for support and told *Terry Willesee Tonight* that her daughter was being brainwashed by The Centre of Knowledge and Supremacy. In a subsequent program after her murder, Dr Kroy made no secret of the fact that he regarded his former wife as evil.

An insight into Dr Kroy's views on those who had left the group is described by a former member who went into hiding after leaving. In a letter to this woman, Dr Kroy wrote, 'Perhaps you will choose to kill yourself to escape a worse death, but your death will be only the beginning. Being a demonic bitch, you will face yourself for a period of time which will seem to be an eternity.'[2]

The same year, Talli met another cult member by the name of Graham Kinney. She described the meeting as a turning point in her life. 'He was melancholy and gentle and we became friends,' she said. 'I joked: I might marry you to get away from my mother.' She was 15 at the time. Soon after turning 16, she and Graham travelled to the Atherton Tablelands in North Queensland, where Dr Chiappalone had re-established The Centre of Knowledge and Supremacy.

On January 1988, with the blessing of her father, Talli married Graham. Their happiness was short-lived. Graham became ill and the couple returned to Melbourne for treatment. They moved in with Dr Kroy, who had a house in

Eltham, a leafy outer suburb of Melbourne and an area popular in artistic and academic circles. On the morning of 24 February, Graham and Talli were informed that Graham had chronic myeloid leukemia and a life expectancy of from three to five years.

That same morning, Gilli returned from Israel, where she had been staying with her sister for six weeks. Prior to her departure for Israel, she had told me that she hoped the time in Israel with her family would give her the opportunity to rejuvenate herself and return to continue the battle. On her return, she found an envelope. Typed in red ink was the address where her ex-husband and daughter were staying in Eltham.

It is alleged that as Gilli drove towards the property, Talli heard her husband scream, 'She's here! I've just seen the car!' In a statement to police Kinney said he was screaming because Gilli was going to get her daughter, Kinney and Dr Kroy as well.

Within minutes of leaving the car she was shot dead, her body mutilated by five close-range blasts from a pump-action shotgun.

At the time Dr Kroy could not be contacted but provided an interview to an Israeli newspaper in which he gave his version of what happened. He confirmed that his daughter had been married at sixteen, the minimum age in Victoria, in order to further remove her from Gilli. The man who had been charged with Gilli's murder was Talli's new husband. Dr Kroy denied the existence of a cult and claimed his former wife was the victim of a mental disease.

I will never forget that Wednesday. I will never forget my visit the following day to Gilli's apartment, where I found Talli's name attached to her 'Tehillat Hashem' prayer book. She had told me she prayed every day for Talli. The police requested that I view the body in order to ascertain whether the pattern of the bullets resembled a ritual killing but the motive was already obvious. I cleared out Gilli's apartment in the hope that one day I would be able to present Talli with Gilli's possessions, in particular, thousands of happy family photos.

Two weeks later, Kinney appeared in the Supreme Court, and it was stated that 'Mrs Kroy had been brutally executed'. Kinney was remanded in custody, where he finished a book titled *And they call me crim: An exposé of our rotten judicial and penal system.* Eventually the book was published by a Mr Roger Smith, another member of the cult. In an epilogue he refers to Kinney as 'an agent of the Supra-Mental Consciousness who was sent incognito to plant the energy bombs which will blow these [judicial and penal] systems apart'.

On 22 December 1988, Kinney was found in a virtual coma, having taken a drug overdose. A legal battle ensued in which Talli went to the Supreme Court seeking an injunction forbidding an operation that would keep her husband alive. She claimed that her husband would not want to be kept alive under such circumstances. Mr Justice Fullagar, in what has become a landmark judgment, said that under Victorian legislation, he could not order doctors to refrain from saving a person's life. The operation went ahead, but Kinney never regained consciousness and died on Christmas morning.

In early 1989, Dr Kroy travelled to Israel on a lecture tour. He failed to show up at one of his talks. Police investigated and found his body in a rented Tel Aviv apartment. They said he had died from an overdose of prescribed drugs.

Meanwhile, in Melbourne, police were of the opinion that Kinney had not acted alone in Gilli's death. And they were confounded by the mystery of the letter which led her to her death. Literally thousands of typewriters were tested, but none matched the red ribbon which sent Gilli to her death. At the inquest, the coroner could only say 'Mrs Kroy had been killed by Graham Kinney, who in turn died of leukemia and complications of his suicide bid'. As Ian Mackay, writing in a Melbourne newspaper, concluded, 'Cosmic forces had been ruled out.'[3]

Gilli's death is tragic evidence of three important lessons. Firstly, that the authorities in this country and others have, as yet, failed to grasp the seriousness of the cult phenomenon and their need to heed the advice of those who do know and understand. Secondly, that seemingly benign groups wield enormous power over their followers to the extent that 'Though shalt murder' is just another commandment.

And thirdly, that intelligence, professionalism and public status are irrelevant in the face of planned and orchestrated mind control. At the time of his death, Dr Kroy was a senior lecturer in philosophy at La Trobe University in Melbourne. He had written numerous books and was highly respected. His prominence both in Australia and Israel was so widespread that both his death and Gilli's received front-page coverage, plus in-depth features right across the Israeli press.

CHAPTER 5

THE ENTRY PROCESS

Mary Garden, whose disenchantment with Christianity led her towards the East, wrote as she landed in India, 'I glanced down at the book that I was clutching on my lap. On the cover was the strange face of Sai Baba which was mopped by black frizzy hair that his devotees likened to a halo. I felt my heart beating. I had tasted the drug of "spiritual love" and had immediately become addicted.' [1]

One of the myths about the cult phenomenon is that people *join* cults. The suggestion that people join cults is as absurd as the idea that people decide to become drug addicts.

> Cults are not merely weird groups that crazy people find attractive. Cults are massive, enduring cons. Although individuals may join cults during periods of stress and demoralization, most cult joiners are more or less within the normal range psychologically. *They do not join groups because they have made a rational and informed decision that these groups will benefit them. They join because they are seduced through a gradual step-by-step process of deceit and manipulation designed to advance the leader's objectives, regardless of the harm caused to members.*

> The centrality of sustained, exploitative manipulation
> distinguishes cults from benign new movements and
> mainstream religions.[2]

What is an 'informed decision'? In order to make an informed decision, a person requires information about the matter at hand, as well as free choice with which to evaluate this information. The problem we have in relation to the cult phenomenon is that both criteria are not present simultaneously. At the time of entry into a cult, the individual can generally claim to have freedom of choice. S/he is not the subject of psychological manipulation nor is s/he being mind-controlled. However, s/he lacks detailed information about the group. Issues of financial contributions, family contact, fund-raising or witnessing requirements are rarely discussed in the early days of cult involvement. Thus, for example, there is no mention that the initial membership fee has little in common with required future commitments. There is no discussion regarding restrictive contact with the family or the harsh cult doctrine.

Indeed, many cults operate under numerous names, which would appear to have no relation to the central group. On numerous occasions I have heard the comment, 'If I had known that the Hunger Project was an arm of the est organisation, I would not have supported it. How was I to know that the Citizens' Commission on Human Rights is connected to the Church of Scientology, or that the Collegiate Association for the Research of the Divine Principle (CARP) is an organisation under the control of the Unification Church — which is another name for the Moonies?'

In their slick advertising, cults present smiling faces and happy families. Some organisations go out of their way to attract prominent personalities, actors and performers. These people are put on centre stage as the cult attempts to broadcast its message to the vulnerable and the unsuspecting public. John Travolta, Anne Archer and Priscilla Presley are part of Scientology's posh celebrity centre.

When one enters a cult, no mention is made of the fact that unless you are a member you are evil, satanic or unworthy of living. No mention is made of the hierarchical nature of cults, whereby the leaders are the beneficiaries of the lower members' hard labour. Mention is not made of the estates, the properties, the sheer wealth of many of these organisations and their leaders, their business interests and their sophisticated marketing programs.

By the time the individual has accessed at least some information of this type, the level of freedom of choice is questionable. The term 'love bombing' has been used to describe the intensive, emotionally laden approach with which the Moonies recruit new members. The result is the clever and subtle creation of a new sense of belonging and security, as well as the promise of happiness and salvation, which cement the relationship between the cult member and the organisation.[3] This takes place well before there has been the opportunity to assess the philosophy or doctrine of the cult.

The issue is also relevant in relation to the rights of parents, individuals or counsellors to intervene (a topic which will be discussed later). The most common criticism of any intervention is the argument that the individual is an adult with a mind of their own, who has made an informed decision to join a particular group. However, it is difficult to support the notion that a cult member has made an informed decision if the relevant information was not available at the time of joining.

The cults are working in a climate which, by its very nature, lends support to their success. In the same way that disillusioned and dispossessed people will support extremist groups and views, the cults are able to capitalise on the weaknesses of society as well as a perceived inability of the established religions and recognised churches to address the individual's spiritual needs, personal problems and dilemmas — as well as global political unrest and conflict.

Cults paint a picture of a perfect world. They stress the contrasts between this perfect world and the dirty political and military scenery around the world. They highlight the fact that religion has failed in its efforts to bring peace and stability. In the eyes of the cult, most conflicts have a religious base, which fuels them at enormous costs of misery and human suffering.

And the initial contrast with this dark picture is striking. In my earlier days of researching the cults, I recall the serenity of the Hare Krishna temples, and feelings of transcendence at the Siddha Yoga ashrams. The messages were about equality and universal brotherhood.

The concept of a living leader, guru or master is a welcome contrast to the more abstract nature of church leadership. A human manifestation of God is far more real than a God 'out there somewhere' or one who supposedly is ever-present in every human being. A tangible leader is real and carries meaning. Today, seeing is believing.

PART 2

WHAT DO THE CULTS BELIEVE?

- CULTS AND BELIEF SYSTEMS

- FUNDAMENTALISM AND EXCLUSIVITY

- 'SUFFER THE LITTLE CHILDREN'

- LYNETTE PHILLIPS BURNS HERSELF TO DEATH

- THE POWER OF MONEY

- CLAIRVOYANTS, PSYCHICS AND FORTUNE TELLERS

- SATANIC CULTS

- THE APOCALYPSE, ARMAGEDDON AND THE END TIMES

As I began to research the various cult groups, it became clear that they encompass a broad range of ideologies and philosophies. My early impressions had been drawn from media reports. At that time, to me a cult was made up of saffron-robed devotees who played music in the city square and asked people for donations.

I assumed that these groups all followed gurus and masters who were living in India or high up in the Himalayan mountains.

Cults conjured up images of chanting, meditation, vegetarian diets and celibacy.

It came as somewhat of a shock to discover that my definition of a cult hardly scratched the surface of this relatively new phenomenon. I learned that there were numerous groups which did not display any of the above imagery but, nevertheless, were destructive and dangerous.

I found out that quite apart from the better-known Eastern cults, there were numerous Christian groups which gave serious cause for concern. There was a growing number of personal development groups attracting attention because of their methods of recruiting and maintaining the trainees in their grasp.

As my client base began to grow, I was amazed to find that the followers of these movements were not just the 'down and out', but seemingly well-adjusted and successful members of the community. The belief systems of these organisations were as relevant to the university lecturer as they were to the untrained labourer.

I discovered that many clairvoyants, psychics and fortune tellers were using the same methods employed by the cults. It was clear that there were no government controls to curtail these people's activities or to make them accountable.

Many of these operators used the notion of repressed memory syndrome, which has generally been discredited.[1] It relies on the theory that under the right conditions people will recognise various forms of abuse which happened earlier in life but have since been forgotten or denied.

The more I learned about cults, the more I understood about the divergence of their beliefs. But, ironically, the more I understood about the divergence of their beliefs, the more I was able to recognise that they all employ similar methods of mind control and psychological manipulation.

CHAPTER 6

CULTS AND BELIEF SYSTEMS

Anne Hamilton-Byrne, leader of The Family cult in Victoria, used to house a multitude of cats in special houses at the back of her property in Ferny Creek. These cats were reincarnations of humans who had not learned the wisdom of her spiritual path. This instilled in the members of The Family the fear that if they deviated from the path, they too would end up in the cattery.[1]

'There are now thousands of people world-wide coming together as one biological body — who feel that death is no longer inevitable. We have created a new agreement in our bodies — with a passion for each other, we create an intimacy and aliveness that goes past death. People Forever of Australia consists of immortals who have made the human being more important than any beliefs or issues that may ordinarily separate us from another ... We are here to end aging, disease and death of the human flesh.'[2]

The term 'cult' has become a household word. Musicians and singers, even politicians, are reported to assume 'cult-like' status and attract huge followings. 'Cult personalities' include sports heroes and Olympic medallists. But when we start talking psychological manipulation and mind control, the word 'cults' takes on a specific meaning.

Cults are not necessarily religious groups. Broadly speaking, they can be divided into a number of categories.

EASTERN GROUPS

The Eastern groups generally adopt a mystical approach to life, although their practices can vary from celibacy and abstinence in some groups to licentiousness and sexual permissiveness in others. In Hare Krishna, sexual contact is permitted only within marriage and is subject to a highly regulated set of laws. In Rajneesh, where the leader Bhagwan Shree Rajneesh has stated that 'sex is the first rung towards enlightenment', there are few if any restrictions on sexual contact between members, be they in a relationship or not.

The Eastern groups are better known for their colourful attire, name changes and different diets. Some groups preach a vegetarian diet whilst others are stricter, insisting on vegan food only. The initiation into the organisation, something which is characteristic of most groups, is often a very colourful ceremony at which the disciple or follower is given a new name and possibly a new birthday as well.

Many of these groups speak about reincarnation, the role of the soul in the destiny of human beings and the nature of our spiritual connection with the higher worlds. Meditation and yoga are emphasised, and chanting and fasting are part of the lifestyle. These characteristics, as well as a bias towards mysticism, continue to make the groups very attractive to Westerners, many of whom become involved whilst travelling through Asia.

The Eastern groups include organisations such as Siddha Yoga, Sahaja Yoga, Hare Krishna, Rajneesh, Divine Light Mission, Healthy, Happy, Holy Organisation (3HO), Soka Gakkai, Meher Baba Organisation, Ananda Marga and Sai Baba.

CHRISTIAN GROUPS AND 'FRINGE CHURCHES'

Apart from the Eastern-oriented groups, which have caught the attention of the public and the media, there are numerous

Christian-based groups which have also been a cause of concern.

These Christian-based groups, sometimes also referred to as 'fringe churches', have attracted attention because of their dogmatic nature and degree of discipline. Dress codes, sexual conduct, prayer and tithing requirements, as well as moral standards, are heavily regulated. As compared the chanting of the Eastern groups, speaking in tongues, which is a feature of some fundamentalist groups, is also prevalent amongst some fringe churches. The implanting of fear in the minds of members acts as a disincentive to leave, even during times of personal crisis. The financial contributions in terms of tithing, as well as the rewards, which are supposedly provided through these contributions, remain a cause for serious concern.

These groups believe that they alone are responsible for the ultimate salvation of the world and that their organisation is the only medium through which this dream will be realised.

Many of these Christian groups fit within the definition of a cult in terms of their structure and operation. Others appear less cult-like. Nevertheless, their agendas are no less destructive or dangerous. These groups are discussed in more detail in the following chapter.

COMBINED GROUPS

In his book *The Lure of the Cults*,[3] Robert Enroth, Professor of Sociology at Westmount College (Santa Barbara), lists a category of cults which combine strands from several religions. The Moonies or Unification Church, for example, is a combination of Eastern philosophy and Christianity. So too are groups such as The Church Universal and Triumphant, and Eckankar. In Australia, the Anne Hamilton-Byrne sect, which has received prominent attention since 1983, practised a combination of yoga, Hinduism, Buddhism and Christianity and was led by a woman who believed she was a reincarnation of Christ.

PERSONAL DEVELOPMENT AND PSYCHO-THERAPEUTIC GROUPS

In contrast to both the Eastern and Christian-based groups, the personal development and psycho-therapeutic groups appeal to the 'me generation'. Many of these groups offer substantial benefits to the participants. Professionally run groups focus on a range of issues, including interpersonal relationships, social interaction, business acumen, goal setting and career issues

However, participation in these groups can create problems when the motives of the organisers are not clear or the group fails to reveal its real agenda. Often, at the expense of marriages and relationships, the individual will grasp the opportunity presented by the group to find out 'who I am and what makes me tick'. Ironically, the individual believes he is regaining his independence and autonomy without realising that the very means by which this is being achieved is subservience and subjugation to a group with questionable motives.

It is not uncommon for relationships to break up when one partner is involved in the organisation, because of the contradiction between the notion of 'me and my self-discovery' and the concept of a relationship. I have counselled numerous couples where the involvement of one partner appears to have contributed to a marriage problem. There appears to be a similarity between many of these cases — a partner very preoccupied with self-development and clearly emphasising this process as a priority over and above the relationship or marriage.

Unlike many of the Eastern groups which appear to attract people in their twenties and thirties, the psycho-therapeutic and personal development groups often attract people in their forties and fifties. One possible explanation is that these groups appear well-placed to offer a response to people who are experiencing their mid-life crisis and who have come to the realisation that life is passing them by, that they may never be the millionaires or the public figures they once set out to be. Women who have reared families and who are no longer needed at home, who married early and never really experienced 'growing up and being free' have found themselves being drawn towards these organisations.

The effects of joining these groups can be all-consuming. It is quite common for members to become ambassadors for the groups, broadcasting the message to friends and family about how their lives are changing for the better. Friends complain about the obsessive and selfish nature of these members with whom there is little left to talk about other than the group.

A further concern regarding many of these groups is expressed by Louise Samways in her book *Dangerous Persuaders*.[4] Samways lists a number of groups, including est as well as other groups, such as Money and You and the Hoffman Process. She expresses concern about the pace of change these groups facilitate, the lack of informed consent on the part of their participants, as well as their misuse of psychological techniques allied to hypnosis in order to bring about the behavioural changes.

OTHER GROUPS

And finally there are groups which practise the occult, as well as others who believe in UFOs and extra-terrestrial or astral connections. It is disturbing to see these groups on the rise. The philosophy of the Order of the Solar Temple included the belief that the suicides for which it is known were connected with continued life on the star Sirius.

CULTS AND POLITICS

A number of cults have managed to incorporate a political agenda into their belief system and philosophy. In the USA the Moonies attract prominent names in the political and academic spheres by hosting international conferences. In 1975 Rev. Moon purchased the *Washington Times* in order to increase his political influence. The Aum Shinri Kyo cult plans to set up a shadow ministry in Japan in order to become an independent nation.

In Australia the Citizen's Electoral Council, which represents the highly racial and anti-Semitic LaRouche movement in the USA, continues to target political and community leaders.[5] The Natural Law Party, which fielded candidates in the 1993 Australian federal election, is closely connected with Transcendental Meditation.

The Ananda Marga movement is aligned with a political philosophy known as Prout, which is actively involved in trying to bring about social reform. From Australia, Ananda Marga attracted international attention because of the alleged connection between the group and the suicide of a young Sydney woman by the name of Lynette Phillips. This tragedy is covered in a separate chapter.

Ultimately, whether a group should be labelled a cult involves a close assessment of the methods, the philosophy and the agenda of the movement. It would be dangerous to form an opinion on the status of any group without making a thorough investigation into these three aspects.

CHAPTER 7

FUNDAMENTALISM AND EXCLUSIVITY

Exclusivism and elitism combined with wrong or unbalanced spiritual warfare teaching become a dangerous cocktail. Family members or friends who put together another point of view are 'demonised' and seen as 'the enemy' or at best 'misled or unenlightened'. The command 'to honour your father and mother' is rationalised away.[1]

Some fringe churches may admit to their fundamentalist nature, but reject out of hand any suggestion that they are cult-like. Yet the nature and behaviour of these organisations calls for closer examination and assessment.

These groups include the Family of Love (formerly Children of God), The Love Family (or Church of Armageddon), The Faith Assembly, Jehovah's Witnesses, The Way International, The Boston Church of Christ, Jews for Jesus, and Marantha Christian Ministries. Other groups that draw attention include the Exclusive Brethren, The Way International, 'The Walk', The Grace Church and Potter's House.

Unsuspecting people are often drawn to these movements because they present as Christian groups which on the surface appear to offer a more progressive form of service and devotion. Often, within a short period of time, dreams are shattered and families destroyed.

'The essential feature of these movements is a claim to be better than other Christians or to be true believers.' As a corollary, the leader or leaders believe they have been called by God to be a vehicle of special blessing to others, having received a special 'vision' or 'revelation' from God.[2]

These distinctions between members and non-members allow groups to operate with a pseudo-superior attitude. An example of such elitism is found within the Jehovah's Witnesses. 'The Jehovah's Witnesses invite everyone to experience the joy that comes not only from having found a religion that surpasses all others but from having found the truth.'[3]

The members' conviction that the leader has been called by God creates a spirit of elitism and separatism, resulting in the belief that only the group and its membership have the right to speak on behalf of Christianity. No one else. Furthermore, because the leader has been called by God, his word is considered divine, regardless of whether it has a biblical origin.

As a result of growing interest in a fringe church called the Order of St Charbel and led by Mr William Kamm, also known as the Little Pebble, the Archbishop of Melbourne, George Pell, issued a statement in June 1997. In the statement he made it clear that the Little Pebble, his teachings and his communities have no approval of the Archdiocese of Melbourne: 'Messages are alleged to have been received from this person in which great emphasis is placed on milleniallism, warnings, signs, torments, days of darkness. Alleged private revelations are given importance above the revealed teaching of Scripture and the authentic guidance of the Church. Messages which are not consistent with the word of God and the constant teaching of the Church are to be rejected.'

For fundamentalist fringe churches the world is divided into two distinct categories: the members of the group, who are the true and only believers, and the outside world, which is branded evil and satanic. People are either part of the group or not; there are no in-betweens. This is the ultimate struggle between good and evil.

In order to reinforce their power and influence, many groups impose a code of secrecy. Members' contact with outsiders is restricted and in some situations cut off altogether. The maintaining of contact with outside family members represents a contradiction to the insular standards of the group. The penalty for contact with outsiders is very often total excommunication. Similarly, any questioning of the group is dealt with harshly, often with public condemnation.

Ron Hemry was 19 when he was caught smoking and thrown out of the Exclusive Brethren. He claims that apart from one ten-minute meeting, he was cut off from his family since being excommunicated. In an interview he said that he didn't even know if his mother, aged 94, was still alive: 'Even now, I would be more than willing to have contact with my mother, if she is still alive, and my sisters, but I know the church would not approve of them doing that ... it is a situation of being brainwashed to the point of not thinking.'[4]

In many fringe churches, control over the membership is absolute. Members' relationships are controlled; the leadership has the final say regarding accommodation and vocation. In addition, adherence to the group is reinforced by strict requirements for confession. Whereas the followers are required to expose their vulnerability, the leaders assume the persona of perfect beings. Furthermore, they encourage the followers to trust them rather than themselves, thereby disempowering them even more.

Invariably, the control of the church extends to the financial commitment of the members. In Melbourne, a support group was established in 1993 to assist former members of an organisation called The Grace Church. Spokesperson for the group, Genna Piraino, claimed that he had lost $200,000 after he unwittingly donated money to the church's leader, Reverend Niel Thomas. 'I even sold my country property, giving him the entire proceeds so they could build a college. It was never built.'[5]

Reverend James Ridgeway, Principal of Kingsley College, said that Reverend Thomas had left a trail of 'broken people, used and disillusioned, if not discarded'. He claimed that the Reverend Thomas's activities should be condemned by fellow Christians because of the patent and continual unethical practices which characterise aspects of his leadership.[6]

Many of these groups have a language of their own with strong emphasis on the subjective experience. There is undue stress on 'words from the Lord', 'God showed me', 'the Lord told me', and 'I sense the Spirit'.[7]

The group keeps its following on its toes by creating a 'crisis mentality' suggesting that the end-times are near, that soon there will be a showdown between good and evil and that only the group will survive the showdown.

In May 1998, William Kamm, leader of the Order of St Charbel, warned his followers that many wars would break out soon and that this would be in preparation for the great war that lies waiting to engulf the whole earth. 'Be not afraid to sacrifice your lives; be not afraid to give of yourself to God.' Mr Kamm preached that there would be two wars, that the army would come and take away the women and children, and that the warriors would have to be prepared to be martyrs. A former member claimed, 'We all believed him. I went out and bought a crossbow with a sight on it, and I was one of the last people to arm themselves.'[8]

In many of these groups, the attitude to women is very oppressive. Very often, women are not involved in the actual service or the process of decision-making; their role is to serve the male population. Women carry second-rate status and are exploited by the male leadership. William Kamm justified his right to have sex with his 'queens' by explaining that the Virgin Mary had suspended the normal rules of adultery for him. In January 1998, he delivered a letter excusing his adultery by claiming that Pope Innocent III allowed it.

Many of these churches enjoy tax-exempt status and other government benefits. But despite the clean image that they attempt to portray, the long-term damage perpetrated by them cannot be underestimated. As Ronald Enroth writes in his work *Churches that Abuse*, 'Unlike physical abuse that often results in bruised bodies, spiritual and pastoral abuse leaves scars on the psyche and soul.'[9]

Ex-members of fringe churches, like other former cult members, often have difficulty in explaining how difficult it is to escape the influence of the group. Mr and Mrs Ken Wallis left the Exclusive Brethren in February 1998, after becoming disenchanted with the church. They took with them their four youngest children, but their four oldest daughters decided to stay with the church and have since cut off all contact with their parents. 'If you have not been part of the Brethren, you cannot understand what it is like,' Mrs Wallis said. Mr Wallis said that he would not give up the quest to have his daughters back. 'We love them very, very much. They have been told that we are evil but we have never done anything wrong and never will,'[10]

CHAPTER 8

'SUFFER THE LITTLE CHILDREN'
— Life Inside the Exclusive Brethren

Ron Fawkes runs a successful furniture business in Australia. He works hard, travels frequently and has a wide social circle. What puts Mr Fawkes apart from his friends is the fact that despite strenuous efforts, he has not seen his ex-wife or his six children since 1984. That was the year he was excommunicated from the Exclusive Brethren, a Christian fringe church with centres in the USA, Britain, New Zealand and Australia.

Mr Fawkes' 'crime' was his outspokenness and criticism of the increasing power of the Brethren's international leader, US-based Jim Symington. 'I believed the world leader was coming between the Brethren and Christ. He has the final say on everything — from whom you will marry to decreeing the amount of milk girls must drink every day. The control he had over people's life was becoming too extreme.'[1]

Mr Fawkes was no newcomer to the Exclusive Brethren. He had been a senior member of the group, stating that he was responsible for dealing with lawyers in cases where action was taken to recover children. In one instance, Mr Fawkes was in court for six weeks trying to keep children away from parents who were no longer in the group. 'When the Brethren claim that they do not split families, it is not true. I was instrumental in breaking up families.'[2]

The Exclusive Brethren broke away from the better-known

religious group, the Plymouth Brethren, in the late 1940s. Members are required to live by a strict set of rules. They are barred from contact with any members who do not comply with the rules. If the matter is not resolved, the member is excommunicated. Although the rules appear to change from time to time, they involve a long list of highly restrictive laws.

Dress codes are strict. Men are not permitted to have moustaches or beards and must have short hair. Women are not allowed to cut their hair, must not wear trousers and must wear scarves on their heads in public.

The group forbids the use of television, radio, computers and CD players. They meet in special halls that usually do not have windows. There are no clocks in the building because the Brethren do not believe that meetings should be governed by time.[3]

Former members allege a string of draconian rules which were binding on the membership, including no picnics, smoking, parachuting, competition or school camps. Pets or guard dogs were not allowed; honeymoons or staying at motels was strictly forbidden.

Perhaps the most disturbing aspect of the Brethren is a primary principle of the church that the word of the leadership is equivalent to the authority of Scripture. It makes no difference whether the edict or instruction actually has a source in Scripture. Hence, as far as the membership is concerned, excommunication is divinely prescribed, regardless of the nature of the offence.

Mr Fawkes says that there is therefore no point in asking the leadership for a biblical source for the prohibition of wearing short pants, having a cup of tea with friends, going for a holiday or doing a night school course. These are offences which lead to excommunication by virtue of the leadership's command.

Members are bound to reveal the names of any people who break the rules of the church, often presenting embarrassing reports to group meetings. A former New Zealand MP, Nick Smith, claimed former members admitted to him that they used to 'confess and repent' regardless of whether they had done the crime.⁴ Mr Smith's claims related to his own investigation into the Brethren in the face of serious and disturbing complaints about the group from his constituents.

Mr Fawkes believes that, like many other fringe churches, the Brethren have doctored the Bible to suit their needs. He says that the group uses the apostle Paul's instruction to Timothy to separate from evil as a justification for the parting of families if a member has left the Brethren. But Mr Fawkes says that this literal interpretation of a single Scripture passage can be offset against numerous other texts with contradictory messages: 'Like most cults, the Brethren have plucked one Scripture out of the context of the whole and rammed it against every other Scripture.' In that respect, Mr Fawkes says that the position of today's Brethren bears no resemblance to the godly beginnings of the early Brethren. The degree to which the rules are constantly changing at the whims of the church's leader helps define the group as a cult.

The absolute control over the members is reinforced by the stringent isolationist policies of the movement. Mr Fawkes claims that the need to isolate members of the Brethren from outsiders is so pronounced that, in Britain, Brethren living in tenement housing with shared interior walls have now been forced to ensure there is a 5mm gap separating them from the adjoining home.

Even more pronounced is the refusal of the Brethren to inform outsiders of the well-being of members of the group. Former members talk of being informed about family deaths months after the occurrence. In one reported case, a husband was separated from his wife when she remained in the Brethren. Three months later his wife died, but he was not informed of her death until nine months later, when he was checking to see where the divorce proceedings were up to.[5]

Mr Fawkes finds it difficult to describe the effects of excommunication. 'It's far worse than being thrown out by your own family. The level of guilt is indescribable and the need to find acceptance is simply overwhelming. Suddenly, you are out on your own in an evil world with no place to go. There is an intense desire to be re-accepted by the group, even though you are aware that it no longer has anything to offer you. Those feelings don't go away; it takes courage to overcome this enormous challenge. Knowing that your children are still there means that ultimately you remain attached to the church.'

Mr Fawkes has to rely on rumours and 'leaked information' in relation to his children. He has been told that three of them have married and had children of their own. 'People leave the Brethren and they come out and tell you things. I have a lot of grief and a lot of pain and, in some ways, most of me is still with the Brethren. Every day I ache for the children; I do not even know what the youngest ones look like.'

The Brethren deny the assertion that they split families, claiming they uphold the family unit tenaciously. Brethren members Bruce Jackson and Bill Wallis reject claims that the group is governed by strict bizarre rules. Instead, they claim they represent 'persons who take the ground of believers in the Lord Jesus, who have come under the efficacy of His finished work to live a different life from what the world lives, as provided for in the fullest way by divine grace'.[6]

In the face of documented accounts of split families and divided relationships, it is difficult to accept the truth of these claims. They would be more plausible if Mr Fawkes were allowed to see his children and if they were encouraged to see him. Until then, the claims of the Brethren ring very hollow.

CHAPTER 9

LYNETTE PHILLIPS BURNS HERSELF TO DEATH

'So please know that I am happy. I don't expect you to be able to accept, but please try to understand ... I have a chance to do something great with my life — what Ananda Marga is will become apparent in the next couple of years ...

'So it seems that my years of prayer have been answered. Finally, I understand why I could never settle and accept the lifestyle all around me. I just wanted something else ... Oh Mum, I'm so excited, like a young plant just beginning to explore the soil and rain and sunlight.'[1]

Lynette Phillips was born in February 1954. Her parents divorced when she was six years old, and she lived with her mother, Mrs Millie Phillips, a successful Sydney businesswoman. She was also deeply attached to her father, Mr Harold Phillips, who was likewise in business in Sydney.

Although her school years were marred by her family situation, Lynette gained a very high pass in her Higher School Certificate and qualified for medicine at the University of New South Wales. She dropped out after a few months.

Lynette was an intelligent, idealistic young woman. In her effort to find meaning in her life, she crossed paths with the drug scene. She also became a vegetarian and eventually, in 1975, joined the Ananda Marga group.

Her troubled background and idealistic nature are, perhaps, best illustrated by the moving suicide note which she wrote prior to her death in 1978. In this note, which was headed 'An Open Letter to All Jewish People', Lynette referred to her background and the fact she was brought up with ever-constant reminders of the Holocaust, tales of lost relatives and destroyed dreams. She wrote that her mind was filled with a fear of living and an unwillingness to risk greatness.

Lynette refers to humanity as one, claiming that each person, regardless of race, has a right to live where they choose and in full dignity. She concludes by saying, 'Fight for the freedom of all people. When that is established, there will be no more war.'

It is understandable, as Mrs Phillips said, that once Lyn got off drugs, she was searching for religion. She had intense conflict, she was restless and trying to find a goal in life. 'She was particularly attracted to the sect, partly because of their social service work. She seemed very content and happy.'[2]

In 1978 Lynette joined Prout, the political arm of Ananda Marga. Prout teaches universalism and is planning active steps to try to show the need for a new world order. Lynette was to die in the name of Prout.

In July 1978, Lynette's father received a letter from her in which she informed him that she had gone to the Ananda Marga's training centre for nuns in Sweden. A few days later he received another letter from her saying that she had taken the plunge to become a nun.

In August, Lynette wrote to her mother from Sweden. In this letter she spoke about her years of pain in dealing with her lack of confidence, family ties and dependencies. She explained how, for four to five years, all her spare time, all her lunch hours were spent in reading spiritual teachings and prayer. 'Coming into Ananda Marga has been like going home — with all the love and struggles of living in a family. Every part of me that was yearning for expression finally had scope and encouragement … I follow Ananda Marga because it is as close to me as my own heart-beat. Yes, there is a need for identification — with a world that is more real than mirrors and advertising.'

On 26 September, Lynette entered Britain. She was carrying a proclamation regarding her own self-immolation. British authorities expelled her after she attempted to burn herself to death outside the British Houses of Parliament in London. Australia House was not informed of her deportation. Later on, Mrs Phillips said she found it extraordinary that British authorities could deport an Australian subject who was quite emotionally disturbed and in a depressed state of mind. The British, in response, claimed that they notified Australian consular officials of the deportation, but that information does not appear to have reached Australia.

According to *The Sun* newspaper, whilst in Britain, Lynette posted a copy of her self-immolation proclamation to the Prout office in Sydney. The Prout secretary acknowledged that it arrived about Friday, 29 September, and that he delivered copies to the newspapers that day. The newspapers did not use the information.

From Britain, Lynette travelled to Switzerland. On 2 October, a woman walked into a petrol station and calmly bought a can of petrol. A woman also rang an international newsagency and said there would be a demonstration outside the busy Place des Nations at 5 p.m. At 4.55 p.m., in protest against the 'inhumanity, injustice and irrationality prevalent in our society', Lynette Phillips quietly sat down, poured petrol over herself and lit a match.

The next morning, news services throughout the world carried the story. *The Age* in Melbourne carried the story as its major front-page report, titled, 'An Heiress Dies: Human Torch Protest'.[3]

A witness to the suicide, quoted in *The Age*, said, 'We were just about to cross the street along the palace grounds to talk to her when all of a sudden she was burning like a torch! It was horrible. She never even cried. There was not a sound out of her. The whole thing lasted only a few minutes.'

Lynette's last testament, her self-immolation proclamation, gave some insight into her motive:

> This act of self-immolation is my own choosing and planned in secrecy. Divulgence would have meant sure prevention. It grew from a burning desire, an inner-need to do something, to help stop the criminality of our exploited lives on earth. It was inspired by the sacrifice of seven others ... whose own sacrifices have not been fully understood by the world. This action is taken to arouse the consciousness among all goodwishing people.
>
> May the light emanated enlighten all other hearts. May this action pave the way for the establishment of a new social order that is devoid of exploitation, misery and injustice.

The proclamation concluded with the hope: 'Wishing you all the glory and prosperity' and was signed, 'Lynette Phillips (Shanti), Proutist Universal Citizen, a lover of humanity.' Next to her signature was the Prout symbol: the rising sun, which represents progress, and the swastika, which represents victory.

A Sydney Prout member, Craig Walter, is reported to have responded to the news of Lynette's death by proclaiming her 'almost a saint': 'Her death was a tragedy, but it was a great sacrifice. She was Australia's first soldier.'[4] A similar view was expressed on an Australian ABC TV program, *Monday Conference*, by the Australian leader of the movement, Acharya Abhiik,[5] who said that Lynette's death was an inspiring act.

On the same program Mrs Phillips, who was in the audience, alleged that what her daughter did 'wasn't what she wanted to do, but what she had to do'. In response, Abhiik tried to compare Lynette's act of self-immolation to the death of Jesus on the cross.

Mrs Phillips also made it clear that all her attempts to contact Lynette through the Ananda Marga offices had been denied.

The issue of self-immolation was discussed in the movement's own publication, *Prout Universal Weekly*, published in Denmark. In the edition of 2 August, published while Lynette was working at the Danish centre, it describes the 'glorious sacrifices' of three Indian members who self-immolated in 1973.[6]

What really happened to Lynette Phillips will always remain a subject of speculation. Did the fact that seven sect members had recently burnt themselves to death affect her? Were her actions a product of her emotional and psychological turmoil, or was Ananda Marga directly responsible? And if it was the internal turmoil, is not Ananda Marga ultimately responsible for not having acted to prevent the suicide, by introducing Lynette to appropriate treatment services?

The fact remains that Lynette was a highly idealistic young woman from a troubled background. Her search for meaning and sense in her life began in her early years. She joined a group which appeared to give her hope, the answers to her prayers.

Other questions remain — in particular, the response of the British authorities to Lynette's first suicide attempt in London. In an article, 'Suicide and Our Sect: For the first time talking in the HQ of Ananda Marga', Garry Barker wrote from

Copenhagen, 'But whatever the justice of the truth, for Lyn the end has come and gone and all that is left is a cinder patch marring a nice green lawn in Geneva.'[7]

I believe the cinder patch extends beyond the grass outside the United Nations in Geneva, to the consciences of all people and authorities that have the power to prevent this type of tragedy and pain from recurring.

Time has shown that the lessons have not yet been learned.

CHAPTER 10

THE POWER OF MONEY

'Many contempory management training schemes have been influenced by the human potential movement which works to 'strip away the societal impact of a personality and get to the core of human goodness'. Unfortunately, for some programs this means trying to expose and re-work people's emotions. In group settings this often requires the violation of personal confidentiality. 'They [the programs] can cause more problems then they solve.'[1]

The past decade has seen the growth of numerous psycho-therapeutic and personal development groups around the world. Australia has been no exception. Whilst many of them offer substantial benefits to the participants, others provide particular reasons for concern.

An organisation which has drawn attention in Australia is Money and You. Originating in the USA, the group claims to offer courses in business management and training. Allegations against it include the fact that participants in the courses become entangled in an organisation which manipulates the mind and capitalises on emotional experiences.

Money and You has attracted clients from both business groups and government authorities. An ABC *Four Corners* program in 1993 documented the participation of the NSW Fire Brigade in Money and You programs. The Brigade said that

28 senior officers and numerous other lower-ranking officers had done the course. Although it admitted that not everybody was satisfied, the course had provided benefits to others.

Some of the officers who had done it were particularly critical. 'It's not for them to attempt to strip away a person's religion or conviction purely with the idea of replacing it with their own,' one officer remarked. 'My observation is that to become part of the dynamics and euphoria which were going on, you had to succumb to their ideas and values. I think the undercurrent of the course is to create a cult following.'

Rev. David Millikan, who investigated the organisation, expressed particular concern about the emotional implications of the group processes. One activity known as the 'blocks game' involved small groups of people sitting around tables. They were given a set of coloured wooden blocks with the objective of organising them in such a way that they represented the emotions of the group. Although the activity may have started out as a benign group experience in the early hours of the evening, this was certainly not the case when at 3 a.m. the groups were still trying to complete the task. With the anxiety and tension rising, it was clear that 'this was a technique to drive people further and further into themselves'.

Millikan claimed that by this time people were becoming so emotional they were losing control of their minds. The level of frustration had them at the breaking point. The room was filled with the sounds of sobbing and screams; virtually everybody was crying. According to one former member, 'Some were on the edge of a nervous breakdown and that's when it really started to worry me. I thought there's more to this than personal development and management style. There was something else which really scared me at the time.'

The program featured graphic scenes of some groups hugging and embracing each other after having found the answer to the blocks game, while others agonised and suffered for not having reached a solution. *Four Corners* was asked to leave the hall at 3 a.m. Millikan claimed that what began as a course in business and planning was now into the world of belief and religion.

Another former member interviewed on the program summed up his views: 'I haven't been subjected to brainwashing but I think if I was, this would be pretty close to what it would be like. Your resistance is lowered to a point where you start losing sight of your own values and your own convictions and of course you're being constantly pounded with these ideas from the people that are presenting the show. The experience was unique. It frightened me. For several weeks I felt I was under assault. I am concerned about some of the people who walk away from the course.'

Other participants in Money and You were more direct in likening it to a cult, claiming that the only effective way of parting company with the group was by exit counselling. One lawyer who had been with Money and You told how he had been prepared to leave his wife and family. The couple had newborn twins and a thirteen-month-old baby. He claimed the group had become part of his business and virtually assumed control of every aspect of his life. He was eventually exit counselled and left the group. 'I wasn't told that NLP [Neuro-linguistic Programming] would be involved. I wasn't told "we are going to put you in a trance and you'll become highly suggestible", he said.

CHAPTER 11

CLAIRVOYANTS, PSYCHICS AND FORTUNE TELLERS

'The fantasy romance [between Princess Diana and Dodi Al-Fayed] is unlikely to last. We will see the Princess spend much more time away from England and her sons. The process of letting go will be very painful. From 1998, the Jupiter and Saturn cycle will provide the opportunity for Princess Diana to settle down to a more serious and stable lifestyle.' (A week before Diana's fatal accident!)[1]

Although cults are usually organised groups with a particular philosophy and set of rituals, there also exist numerous 'one man bands', which lack the organisational structure of the cult but resort to very similar practices. These people can be as dangerous as the cult leaders. They prey on the vulnerable elements of our society, using a range of techniques, including hypnosis, to attract a following.

Several years ago I received a phone call from Nigel. He had been married for nine years to Carol. Both were originally from England but had migrated to Australia shortly after they married. They had two children. Recently she had begun to see Cheryl, a naturopath in a nearby city. 'Since then everything has changed,' Nigel said. 'She seems to have lost all her feelings for me and appears to be spending more and more time with the naturopath. She seems to be turning our daughters away from me.'

In desperation, Nigel's parents came out from England to see the family. During the three weeks they were here, Carol refused to see them. Furthermore, she forbade her daughters to have any contact with them unless Cheryl agreed.

I find that there is a particularly disturbing ring to cases like this. Although it is clear that the techniques and methods used by individuals such as Cheryl replicate the practices of the gurus and the masters, the intensity of the one-on-one relationship can be particularly disconcerting.

In many situations, the follower or disciple feels a unique sense of privilege in being chosen to study under the leader, and is told not to underestimate it. Often the disciple is ecstatic about at last having a personal master.

Because the situation doesn't resemble a cult in terms of its outward appearance, has no name and usually no fixed address, it is difficult to gain an accurate picture of what is going on. Nigel told us that Cheryl practised from a shopfront near their home. But he also noted that Carol was always the last 'patient', and that she would often stay with Cheryl for hours at a time.

There are particularly disturbing aspects in this type of situation, where one person gains control of another person's life.

Hassan refers to the similarities between this situation and the well-known syndrome of battered wives. Drawing from existing research,[2] Hassan refers to the fact that some battered women were forced into nearly totally dependent relationships, being kept away from family or friends who were critical of the relationship. Their self-esteem was slowly eroded as they were denied freedom, money or the opportunity to work. Physical and emotional abuse were common, while the women were made to believe that they were responsible for the marriage problems and anything else which was going wrong.

Such women, though free to leave, don't. Eventually, a point is reached when the mind control is such that there is no need for any physical restriction or boundaries.

In a larger cult, the death of a leader will mean a replacement within a short period of time. Any thoughts that the cult may break up are resolved through the new appointment. After the leader's death, cult members console each other and try to draw strength from the experience. To whom does Carol turn after she is out of those clutches?

Although the case referred to above and the longer case study below are extreme, they are important in that they highlight an increasing need for controls and accountability for psychic healers, clairvoyants or fortune tellers.

Whereas the *modus operandi* of such individuals may not fit all the strict criteria of cults, it often replicates a number of the cult-like processes of mind control and indoctrination. Many of these people's predictions are merely suggestions, which later on serve to modify the person's behaviour, thereby assisting in the fulfilment of the prediction or prophecy. The settings in which they are delivered, the tone of voice and the often ambiguous nature of these messages make it relatively easy for the client to absorb the information and allow it to influence future behaviour. The astrological prediction regarding Princess Diana featured at the beginning of this chapter may have been disregarded by the majority of Australians. However, for those who wanted to read truth into the prediction, it was certainly possible — until discredited by her death a week later!

Another related area of concern involves the use of personal trainers to facilitate spiritual growth or development. In some situations, this may create a bond or sense of obligation towards the trainers when, in fact, they have done little more than empower the people to recognise their own strengths.

Louise Samways, referring to particular healing movements that offer training, writes, 'Basically, you pay to be convinced that you now have a special power when in fact you had it all along. I have no doubt that the "energy" they refer to, which is used by so many different cultures, is real, although it is known by many different names. The Russians have been researching it under the name of bioplasmic energy for many years and believe it is actually the electromagnetic field of the body. The same energy is used in acupuncture. The Hindus call it "prana", the Chinese "Chi".'[3]

CASE STUDY: HOW ONE WOMAN ALMOST DESTROYED A LIFE

'What else can I say except that it was devastating to receive your message. I fail to understand where all your anger and hate is coming from. I am so sad you feel this way. I have always been there for you and I have given you all my support and love. There is nothing else I can give; all I can do is to wait for you.'[4]

Joanna, a 26-year-old woman from Perth, was introduced to Nora, a middle-aged woman living in Northern Victoria, who claimed she was a Buddhist clairvoyant. She was invited to move in with Nora and, within a few months, she had virtually broken off contact with her parents. Within a year, she had made a formal statement against her parents, alleging an extensive litany of sexual abuse. Her life, relationships and outside contacts had been severely controlled. All phone calls were monitored, and she was subjugated to a strict, almost draconian, code of behaviour. Her tasks in the house were humiliating and dirty. She was told that her only means of leading a 'normal' life would be with the guidance of Nora.

Concerned about the influence of Joanna's parents, the pair travelled overseas where they spent a year in India. Almost three years from the time of her original involvement, Joanna was removed from Nora's home as a result of the intervention of the police. She suffered from all the classic post-cult symptoms. It took over a year for her to recover from the experience and get back on her feet.

To complicate things further, after she was removed from Nora's control, Joanna withdrew the statement alleging sexual abuse and was subsequently charged by the police with the offence of making a false statement. The case was taken to court. After the full details of her circumstances were revealed, the court decided to give Joanna a chance to retain her conviction-free reputation.

A closer assessment of Joanna's dramatic story provides a disturbing insight into the potential damage caused by a leader who is allowed to wield extreme power and exercise the very same mind-control practices that exist in the larger and more established cults. In certain respects the dangers may be even more acute.

Joanna was born in Perth in August 1969. When she was nine, her parents divorced. A series of nasty custody battles ensued, complicated by the fact that both parents were now living in different states: her father in Sydney and her mother in Perth. Joanna recalls these times as being extremely upsetting and traumatic as the battles intensified.

Following her completion of high school, Joanna enrolled in an Arts course at Sydney University. The home situation was unsettling and she was assisted by the university in finding emergency accommodation. The pressures continued to build up, and eventually Joanna dropped out of university. At the time she had a Buddhist boyfriend, who encouraged her to read some Buddhist books. Eventually she attended Buddha House, as well as the Chenrezig Institute in Queensland, where she worked as a cook while receiving teaching from the resident lama and Western nuns.

In 1993 Joanna was introduced by a friend to Nora. Her friend had told her about this 'amazing' woman who was teaching her meditation. According to her friend, Nora was a Buddhist teacher of Mahayana Buddhist meditation and a clairvoyant.

Joanna admits that she was experiencing an extremely difficult time in her search for meaning in life. Behind her lay a very messy divorce and numerous unresolved issues with her parents. Spiritually, there was a void in her life which she desperately wanted to fill. Joanna was vulnerable to anyone who would show her some guidance and direction.

Joanna's vulnerability and naivety were further evidenced by the fact that she moved into Nora's house four days after meeting her for the first time. The fact that one 'counselling session' could influence her so strongly was frightening.

'This was the beginning of a two-and-a-half-year experience during which I lost independence, my ability to think freely and my desire to pursue a career. Ultimately it culminated in my actually believing that my parents and numerous other people close to me were sexual abusers and paedophiles. I attribute this absolutely and totally to Nora's desire to manipulate and control me in the most devious of ways and for her own personal benefit. It is only as a result of the intervention of the police and the professional counselling services that I have attended and continue to attend that I have been able to regain my personal freedom and recognise how I was manipulated and controlled.'

It was during her very first counselling session with Nora that Joanna was told she had been sexually abused by a woman in her family. Already under Nora's control, she agreed to take on various exercises in order to 'reclaim' her sexuality. Later on, Joanna recalled that, prior to meeting Nora, she had never thought anybody in her family had abused her. In fact, during the custody battles between her parents, various psychological tests had been conducted, and there were no indications at all of any such abuse. Within days of accepting that her mother had abused her, Joanna was informed by Nora that her father had done likewise and that her step-brother was in danger as well.

Soon after that, Joanna was given a spiritual name. As far as Nora was concerned, this was Joanna's new name. Joanna became Nora's assistant and secretary, and her pay was the counselling and Buddhist teachings given by Nora.

On Nora's instructions, Joanna decided to tell her mother about her knowledge of the abuse. Her mother recommended that Joanna see a qualified counsellor. Nora became furious, declaring, 'The majority of counsellors are more harmful than helpful, they actually promote aggression instead of relieving hurt and are not as enlightened or as good as me.' Joanna was forbidden to see a counsellor.

Nora now began to restrict Joanna's contact with relatives and friends. She also completely reorganised her life. She gave her rosters detailing what time she should get up, the meals she had to cook and the clothes she had to wear. The clothes were designed to make her look older and generally unattractive. There were rules about make-up and how she should do her hair. Nora went through Joanna's possessions and instructed her to throw most of them out, especially those given her by her mother.

Finances were a major issue. Despite the fact that Nora was on a disability pension from Social Security, she continued to charge $80 per session for counselling. She requested that Joanna open accounts at Myers and David Jones. Over a period of time Joanna spent more than $3000 on shoes and clothes, a double bed, a refrigerator and a dryer. Despite being short of money, she tried to keep up payments on these accounts.

In early 1994, on Nora's instructions, Joanna made a formal complaint to the police about her father and stepmother. The statement, which alleged serious sexual abuse, was dictated word for word by Nora. 'Despite the fact that there was absolutely no basis to these allegations, I followed instructions, well knowing that any action against my father and stepmother could seriously harm their professional careers in the fields of public service and education.'

Nora claimed that she was agoraphobic. After moving from Sydney to the Dandenongs in Melbourne, she instructed Joanna to do all the shopping for the house, including personal items such as toiletries and underwear. Doctors came to the house, and Joanna would pick up the scripts. Sometimes she would have to do five or six errands in a day. If she forgot to include something on the list, she would have to go out again, no matter how busy or tired she was. In addition, she was expected to cook, clean and sell Nora's herbal remedies all around Victoria.

Nora's control began to extend to Joanna's boyfriends, with whom she was allowed only limited contact. She claimed that the boyfriends were also sexually abusing her; in one instance she predicted that one of them 'would cut off her right breast'.

In late 1994, Nora instructed Joanna to significantly restrict contact with her mother, saying, 'If you really feel the need to keep in contact with her, limit your phone conversations to a couple of minutes only and gradually break off contact altogether.' A short time later Joanna received an invitation to attend her cousin's wedding in Perth, but Nora refused her permission to go.

In early 1996, the focus turned to money, with Nora suggesting that Joanna send a demand for money to her mother and stepfather, who were then holidaying in Fiji. Nora typed the letter and instructed Joanna to fax it to her mother. The letter demanded an amount of $95,000, threatening that in the event it wasn't paid, the sexual abuse they had perpetrated would be made public. The response to the fax was negative. Joanna's stepfather wrote back, 'I have enclosed a list of offences which you have committed to date. Please take a good look at the periods you can spend in jail before you do anything else. No money.'

In late February 1996, Nora insisted that Joanna make a statement to the police about her mother and stepfather's sexual abuse. Joanna agreed and made an eleven-page statement to the police. It was a bizarre litany of lies, which had no credibility whatsoever. Later on, the police admitted that the outrageous nature of the allegations were enough to convince them that this statement was a fraud.

Shortly afterwards Joanna received a call from a detective who was on his way to Melbourne to interview her. Nora was becoming nervous about the involvement of the police. She became physically abusive to Joanna. At one time she wrenched Joanna's head back by pulling her hair and punched her three times in the cheek. She threatened her with violence and promised to break every bone in her body. During the final three days with Nora, Joanna had one meal.

Completely humiliated and broken down, totally confused and with no strength to resist, Joanna did just one more thing for Nora. She wrote out a statement confessing that she had abused several children, as well as Nora and her son, and that she had attempted to murder her stepmother. She also confessed to being a drug addict.

In early 1996, Joanna was interviewed by the police. The interview was the turning point, being the first opportunity Joanna had in three years to tell her story. Terrified about what

Nora would do to her, she recounted some of the events surrounding her stay with her. She was advised to pick up her belongings and leave. Once back in the house she was assaulted and punched in the ribs by Nora as she desperately tried to defend herself. Nora demanded that Joanna sign over her car, which she did. In the end she was able to leave the house only because the police knocked at the door.

Joanna admits that although she was desperate to get away and feared for her life, 'I would have stayed if she would have asked me to. I was still totally under Nora's influence and would have done anything she asked.'

Once she had left Nora, Joanna commenced the long road towards recovery. She was introduced to me the day after she left Nora. There was no doubt in her mind that she had become a victim to a bizarre form of indoctrination perpetrated by a woman who was prepared to go to any lengths to achieve total control over her disciple.

I worked with Joanna for two years. During that time, she voluntarily participated in an exit counselling program and, despite the terror and the pain which lies behind her, resumed a normal lifestyle. She was reunited with her family, recommenced her studies and became involved in the general social scene. During that time I had regular contact with her and her family. I believe that she was saved just in time and that continued involvement with Nora presented a real danger to her mental health, with a total breakdown not far away.

Exactly one year after she was rescued from Nora's clutches, Joanna faced court on a charge of making a false statement to the police. The magistrate was presented with Joanna's 41-page affidavit, in which she listed the events which had led up to the statement. Her mother and stepfather were present in court. I also attended as a witness.

The magistrate spoke of the seriousness of the charge, accepting the unique and devastating circumstances which lay behind the statement. Joanna's barrister, presented a powerful plea in mitigation of the offence, stressing the punishment that Joanna had already suffered under Nora's influence. Furthermore, the counselling she had undertaken had given Joanna the potential to become a worthwhile and contributing citizen.

Joanna received a non-conviction disposition and walked from the court a free woman. Finally, she was able to reclaim her independence and autonomy, and for the first time in four years, she could look ahead.

CHAPTER 12

SATANIC CULTS

Several years ago a young woman appeared at my office refusing to disclose her identity, she produced a necklace and requested that I hold it, which I did. She asked for it back, but told me she wanted me to know that with that necklace she had just strangled her daughter. She felt she had to tell someone what she had done. Within moments she ran from my office.

Satanism and satanic cults stand apart from many of the other groups for three significant reasons. Firstly, there is a lack of consensus amongst professionals regarding the existence of Satanism and the credibility of the alleged victims. This contrasts with an increasing acknowledgement by most informed health workers and therapists of the existence of the cult phenomenon.

Secondly, the structure of satanic groups differs from the general cult model. Although the notion of leadership exists within the satanic cults, they often lack the strict hierarchical nature and discipline of other cults. Group membership is horizontal in nature, with the strength of the group being its membership. Generally, many satanic cults are very small and operate without central premises or a written doctrine. In this respect, they lack the sophistication of the larger cult groups.

Thirdly, satanic cults are evil. They thrive on evil practices with no regard for the innocence of the victims. They become the forum for a range of psychopathic and sociopathic behaviours. If the allegations of foetal sacrifice and murder are correct, and if the suggestion that these cults involve torture of the most horrific nature are true, there are no adequate expressions of condemnation. Unlike most cults, where the observer admits there may be some elements of good will buried beneath the corruption and manipulation, the satanic cults offer no such comfort.

Cults which are alleged to practice Satanism attract particular attention because of the bizarre nature and extreme behaviour of the members. Reports regarding Satanism make headlines, even though the alleged activity is often unrelated to a particular cult.

Such was the case in the 'Lesbian Vampire Trial', which was heard before the Brisbane court in February 1991 and involved a group of Satan-worshipping women who drank a man's blood after hacking him to death in their evil lust for thrills.[1]

Whether the introductory story of this chapter was genuine is difficult to evaluate. However, it was consistent with what I had heard in the work I had been doing with other members of satanic groups. So great was the trauma associated with this work, that in 1990 several colleagues and I established a support group, so that we could cope better with the problems which were presenting.

It is alleged that satanic cults are involved in extreme and bizarre practices, including the slaughter of young children, as well as perverse sexual practices, including bestiality. Satanic cults are accused of breeding children for sacrificial purposes. The nature of sexual perversity knows no bounds, as has been documented in drawings and illustrations by members of such groups.

Adult survivors have recalled being drawn into black rooms with no windows, with a pentigram drawn on the floor. They recall being surrounded by chanting adults in masks or hooded cloaks, dancing around a hole in the ground from which smoke rose and the 'devil' spoke to them. Former cult members have alleged that on reaching puberty some girls are singled out as 'breeders' to produce foetuses or babies to be used in sacrifices.

In the mid-1980s, a satanic-cult-monitoring group by the name of Tracker was established in the USA by a defence attorney, Bob Shur, and a high school history teacher, Jeff Hilson. Hilson has blamed certain rock music groups which have identified themselves with the occult and Satanism for enticing young people to these practices.[2]

Interestingly, in September 1985, the US Senate approved legislation denying tax exemptions to any cult promoting Satanism or witchcraft. This overrode laws by which these organisations could claim tax-exempt status as religious organisations.

The issue of Satanism remains controversial. Dr Anne Schlebaum, a Sydney psychiatrist, who has counselled many victims of ritual abuse, agrees that people can rationalise these stories by saying children are making them up. 'But there are many children who can't even read, yet are giving detailed descriptions of things like anal rape, pentagrams and animal sacrifice. Either this is an international conspiracy of tots, or children around the world are experiencing ritual abuse,' she says.

At a conference held at the Association of Trauma and Dissociation (AATD) in Melbourne 1997, several health professionals referred to ritual abuse victims being programmed as brothel workers, drug and arms dealers, assassins and fodder for the pornography industry. In Australia, the NSW Sexual Assault Committee has responded with the printing of an information booklet called *Ritual Abuse: Information for Health & Welfare professionals*.

In 1991, Dr Jerry Gelb, an Australian psychiatrist, was first referred patients who claimed they were victims of ritual abuse. Although he says that his initial reaction was grave concern, he believes that the claims were a product of inappropriate therapy by inexperienced therapists who were unintentionally influencing vulnerable patients through the use of leading questions.

Often the process will occur almost unconsciously, and patients enjoy a twofold gain from being labelled victims of ritual abuse. Firstly, the title of 'survivor' gives them a status which makes them more worthy of attention and support. Secondly, the sudden emergence of this dark and inexplicably hidden past can explain longstanding problems.

'If you look at the transcripts of some of these interviews, you'll find that rarely are investigators truly objective,' Dr Gelb explains. 'Just asking a question which may be leading can prompt an affirmative response from a child. And if a person who has not been satanically abused is being encouraged to believe they've been sacrificing babies and eating them or forced to partake of all other kinds of unspeakable acts, that's a totally unacceptable state of affairs.'[3]

The lack of certainty regarding the incidence of Satanism is the subject of an article 'Teen Satanism', by Bob Tucker. He argues that because Satanism is a recent phenomenon attracting little professional attention until now, few objective measures exist. 'We are forced to rely on media coverage of particularly lurid cases, and are forced to rely, as well, on impression by practitioners in the field.'[4]

A more chilling response to the issue and perhaps a telling comment on it comes from the Prosecutor in the case of a Satanist who was found guilty of murder. The Prosecutor, Paul Cummings, in the book *Cults That Kill*, by Larry Kahaner, describes the case as a 'voyage into an underworld we don't want to admit exists in our society'.[5]

CHAPTER 13

THE APOCALYPSE, ARMAGEDDON AND THE END-TIMES

'The fight is over energy and the universe. The evil mind wants to take control of the energy of the beings in the universe. We are now at the time of a final battle when the usurper will be overthrown, the evil ones will be punished, the original plan will be restored ... after the clearing of the planet there will be retraining of those left in the plan for the establishment of the original order.' [1]

The focus of the cults on specific dates for major change or possible catastrophic natural disaster is consistent with the numerous cult philosophies and ideologies. Perhaps the difference between the cults' predictions and those of the established religions is the precision which is attached to the dates — sometimes including even the actual hour at which time the event will take place. The Christian idea of resurrection is not accompanied by a particular date or time. The Jewish Messianic view includes a set of circumstances which will precede the event and even a suggested latest time when this will take place; there is no specific date or time.

In contrast, the Order of the Solar Temple not only referred to the end-time notion, but documents in early 1993 indicated that the cult was preparing to 'transit' into a better world.

The Branch Davidians, who met their fiery death with the destruction of the Waco compound, was a cult fixated on biblical prophecies of disaster and the end of the world. The cult began interpreting weather changes as proof of the coming of Armageddon. A blizzard was regarded as an apocalyptic sign, as David Koresh continued to predict the imminent end of the evil society.

In July 1997, Australian authorities expressed concern about an organisation called the Order of St Charbel in rural Victoria, run by a leader, Mr William Kamm, who calls himself the Little Pebble. Mr Kamm's prophecies included a series of apocalyptic forecasts: the prediction that Perth would be swallowed up because of the sins of the Sodomites and that Sydney would be swallowed up by earthquakes and the atomic bomb. The east coast of Australia would be swamped by the sea ...

In a leading newspaper report, the Catholic Church was reported as having declared Mr Kamm a fake. Kamm, in a 'global press release' sent out in March, told followers to remain inside for seven days, cover windows with black plastic and leave animals outside. 'We believe that before the year 2000, the world will be chastised through a comet — possibly two; then the Pope will leave Rome and die soon after, and a third world war would occur.'[2]

In Russia, a would-be Messiah by the name of Vissarion has managed to attract 5,000 followers to the City of the Sun. According to reports in the Russian press, the leader is a former traffic cop who was fired for his drinking. He speaks of the 'coming end' and instructs believers that suicide is not a sin.[3]

Already in 1973, Herff Appelwaite and Bonnie Lu Nettles, leaders of the ill-fated Heaven's Gate cult, were convinced that they were the two witnesses prophesied by Revelation to prepare the way for the kingdom of heaven. Appelwaite and Nettles claimed to be extra-terrestrial representatives of the 'Kingdom Level Above Human', believing their bodies were mere vessels. By renouncing all worldly pleasures as well as sex, drugs, alcohol, their birth names and all relationships with family and friends, they could become ready to ascend to space, shedding their containers of bodies and entering God's Kingdom.[4]

Cults appear to be able to alter their predicted dates without difficulty. The Church Universal and Triumphant's (CUT) leader, Elizabeth Claire Prophet, was able to revise her dates for the predicted nuclear war with the Soviet Union, which was expected to commence in October 1990. Instead, the group's leader told her followers 'to be concerned and to be prepared for a first strike by the Soviet Union upon these United States', explaining that a twelve-year period was about to unfold, during which the dreaded events could come at any time.

A former vice-president of CUT is quoted as saying that he is convinced that the world is about to enter a decade of nuclear war, earthquake, famine, pestilence and economic collapse. Church members utter high-speed, almost hypnotic chants, praying that the global chaos won't trigger the dreaded 'end-times'.[5]

In Delaware County, Pennsylvania, the Church of First Love was the subject of complaints by residents in relation to the setting up of homes surrounded by high weeds, oil barrels and abandoned cars. Some members of the church were selling their property for a planned move to the wilderness to escape an expected nuclear holocaust.[6]

A potential crisis may exist when the cult leader's predictions fail to eventuate. David Koresh, leader of the Branch Davidians, responsible for the deaths of 83 people at Waco, Texas, in 1993, had forecast a number of events, including a series of natural disasters which failed to materialise. David Clark, Chairman of the Exit Counselling Guidelines Study Group of the American Family Foundation, speculated that Koresh's failure as a prophet might have been a trigger for the Waco disaster. 'When they [the prophesies] didn't occur ... well it's one thing to reject the world, but it's another when you're the one making the predictions and they don't come through,' he said.[7]

Interestingly, failure of a particular prophecy to eventuate may produce the opposite result. A colourful example is cited in Leon Festinger's book *When Prophecy Fails*,[8] regarding a cult in Wisconsin whose leader predicted the end of the world. Claiming to be in contact with aliens, he convinced followers to sell their homes and give away their material possessions. They were then to wait on a mountainside to be picked up by flying saucers before the world was destroyed by a flood the next morning.

When none of this happened, a few followers left. But, in a revealing twist, most of them stayed after having been convinced that the aliens spared Earth from this fate due to the witness of their faithful vigil. Members were feeling more committed than ever to their leader! A group with a very similar belief system is currently operating in Western Australia. Claiming a connection with Sai Baba, an Indian guru with a massive following, it has moved from the city onto high ground and established a self-sufficient community, as they wait for a flood which will engulf the whole country.

Dr Margaret Singer expresses concern regarding groups that preach 'a mix of old-fashioned doomsday predictions, New Age mysticism, radical environmentalism, survivalist philosophy and the narrow world view of identity groups who want to live only with their kind; this transcontinental movement appears to offer inspiration to form utopian communities around a guru, cult leader, survivalist leader, or channeler'.[9]

And in a chilling warning regarding the way these leaders prepare followers for the end-times, the same author concludes, 'We hope such occurrences do not happen, but if they do, let us not call the deaths *suicide*. Let's view them for what they are: the sad, lonely, dreadful ending of life for people who trusted too much, followed too long, and could not get away from a self-serving murderous leader.'[10]

PART 3

CULTS, CHILDREN AND THE MENTALLY ILL

- CULTS AND CHILDREN

- CULTS AND THE MENTALLY ILL

The transition from researching and studying the cults to working with families was not easy. There were very few people in Australia involved in similar work, people I could talk to, places where I could seek advice.

My overseas contacts were invaluable. I also built up a network of former members of various groups who were willing to assist me in my work with families. Although I remained concerned about the injustices being perpetrated by the cults, I had no choice but to accept what I was seeing as a reality along with other social ills of our time and generation.

Far more difficult to accept and even more disturbing was the harm suffered by two particular segments of society — the children and the mentally ill. It was painful to witness and experience the treatment of these often defenceless people at the hands of the cults.

I noted how children were made to feel special, not because of their innate qualities, but because they belonged to the cult.

Children's parenting was often shared with other cult members. Parents' roles were rostered, and their family responsibilities took second place behind their obligations to the cult.

I tried to convince the Family Court that cult-related custody battles were different and deserved special attention. My pleas fell on deaf ears. I once dashed to Sydney airport in a last-ditch effort to convince a mother not to enrol her three infant children in a cult-based Indian school. And I was present at the emotional reunion of a father with his wife and two children after they were successfuly exit-counselled from an Australian cult organisation.

The plight of the mentally ill follower or devotee was equally disturbing. Stripped of powers of rational thinking and emotionally vulnerable, these people were sucked into a system which had nothing to offer them other than a short-term false sense of security and faith. Without appropriate supports or therapy, they became increasingly dependent on the group, only to be thrown out as they became unmanageable.

I watched as a former member of a USA-based cult was certified by the mental health authorities. I read how a former member of the Anne Hamilton-Byrne cult in Victoria was committed to the Larundel Hospital as a result of the cult experience.

Against a backdrop of government inaction and a series of inappropriate responses to cultism, it remains a tragedy and an indictment of our society that these groups are not held accountable and that there is no system whereby they can be brought to justice. Despite the innocence of the children and the mentally ill, they continue to be the targets of opportunist, corrupt and power-hungry groups spreading their tentacles in Australia and around the world.[1]

CHAPTER 14

CULTS AND CHILDREN

'Erhard (the founder of est) sometimes led portions of the children's training and once caused a girl no older than six to break down in tears in front of others. The little girl had been fidgeting nervously while Erhard was talking to a group of children seated in a large circle of chairs.

"'Stop that!" he told the girl brusquely as she wriggled uncomfortably in her seat. For a moment she obeyed his order, but then began fidgeting again, this time laughing a little nervously when Erhard turned to her with a harsh look in his eyes.

"'I said stop that!" he repeated in a rising voice. An angry Erhard grabbed a chair next to him and slammed it down in front of the children, ordering the now-frightened girl to sit on it. "Okay," he told her. "Now start fidgeting." The girl looked up at him with a puzzled look on her face.

"'I told you to fidget." Slowly she began to squirm in her seat. But Erhard was not through with her, demanding that she wriggle even more in front of everyone else. She began to cry and soon the tears were streaming down her face. Erhard kept up his little demonstration for another moment before pulling her off the chair and ordering her to sit outside the circle of children in the room.' [1]

In 1983, Australian community services authorities were notified about the existence of a group of children who had been completely isolated from their families in a cult known as The Family, led by a woman called Anne Hamilton-Byrne. Their hair had been dyed blond, they had been given new names, all carrying the leader's surname as their own.

In her book, *Unseen, Unheard and Unknown*, Sarah Hamilton-Byrne, a former member of the group, wrote. 'We believed the Aunties could kill us because we had been so bad. We didn't know that it was illegal to punish us as they did, let alone kill us. We didn't know there was a society out there that could stop them; that there were any rules apart from theirs. To us they had complete control over life and death.'[2]

In 1992, the same community service authority was involved in a series of simultaneous raids on the Children of God sects in Victoria and New South Wales. A witness involved in the raids said that the Government was concerned about significant harm to the sect children. 'There was a worry that their emotional development may be at risk. They were subject to extreme isolation, which caused them to be deprived of ordinary children's experiences,' the witness said. 'The children had no outside contacts, no recreation facilities and were forbidden contact with extended members of their families, especially those who may have expressed concern about the sect.' The witness said that the children had told her they must smile all the time. 'Crying is not a response these children are allowed,' she said.

In 1996, schools run by the Steiner educational system in Victoria were criticised in the media for cult-like practices. A barrister circulated a letter to parents in May 1996 claiming the Steiner group was similar to a cult. In the letter, a copy of which was obtained by *The Age*, the barrister claimed, 'the Steiner parents had been recruited into an organisation which he compared to the Church of Scientology, the Children of God, Hare Krishna, the Moonies and other cults.'[3]

Overseas, the death of over 300 children in the Jonestown tragedy, as well as some 30 children in the Waco tragedy, shocked the world. Against a backdrop of hundreds of reported cases of child abuse and neglect in cult groups, the vulnerability of children became apparent to the public.

The leader of a Canadian cult called The Science of the Soul urged his followers to blindfold their newborn children until the age of five in order to prolong the children's innate 'purity'. A former devotee said that whilst in the group's ashram in India she witnessed children being forced to meditate ten hours a day in total isolation.[4]

In 1990, six Philadelphian children whose parents were associated with The Faith Tabernacle died of complications from measles. According to a local health official, with one exception, the children could have been saved with medical care.[5]

Although some of these cases may be dramatic, it is difficult to believe they are isolated incidents. The issue of the effect of cults on children is perhaps one of the most emotive, yet painful, realities of the cult scene. In the same way that sick children and children's hospitals strike a special chord, so too does the thought of children whose lives and future are jeopardised by cult influence.

The helplessness and the innocence of children calls for sensitivity and care. The ability to nurture them on their journey to adulthood is a skill which often receives less than due recognition. The thought of this process being prostituted by a self-righteous and self-professing leader is a frightening one.

There will always be divisions in the community in relation to the issue of adults becoming involved in cults. Whether the decision to join was an informed decision, and therefore justifiable, remains a contentious issue. There can be no such argument regarding children, who are either introduced to the cult at an early age or who are born into the organisation.

In addition, where only one parent is involved with the cult, issues of care, custody, residency and guardianship become far more pressing as the non-cult parent faces the prospect of children growing up in a destructive environment.

The pain arising out of these situations knows no bounds. The black-and-white cult distinction regarding those who belong to the organisation and those who don't does not exclude the extended family. The non-cult parent, the grandparents and other relatives are branded as being evil as the young child gropes in the darkness of cult life. Contacts between the child and the extended family are restricted and, in many cases, prohibited altogether.

Even if eventually the child is freed from the movement, with or without a parent, there are no prospects of reliving the critical developmental stages, which have been missed in so far as the non-cult parent is concerned. Like a tree which has been stunted in its early growth, the possibility of normal relationships becomes difficult, if not impossible.

Although various tragedies involving cults have highlighted their perilous effect on children, there are few controls in place to address this issue. Some comfort can be drawn by the existence of child protection authorities under our democratic system, but cults have learnt how to provide adequate responses to inquiries from the authorities.

Although I believe that the primary issues in relation to children in cults relate to the freedom of choice and family relationships, there are other issues unique to this dynamic which are worthy of mention.

They include the fact that many cults reject professional medical care, substituting in its place an absolute ideology that creates harsh discipline. Children may be deprived of adequate health care, including immunisation. Furthermore, the geographical isolation of cults as closed societies often enables them to resist inquiries and investigations into child abuse. The geography of cults also means that the children are brought up in isolation from non-cult youngsters. Their education, if they are allowed to study at all, is totally controlled by the cult leader.

Children in cults will adopt the leader's beliefs or delusions, even in relation to particular phobias or attitudes, which, for example, may label outsiders of the group as evil. Normal development is hindered as children are unable to express their feelings or even show signs of rebelliousness in their infancy.

The cult's hierarchical structure and its view of itself as a family place parents in the position of 'middle managers' with regard to their children, a subservient role which can become especially dangerous when the leader measures the parents' dedication by their willingness to abuse their children at his or her request.[6]

Although there are some studies which provide compelling arguments as to the *possible* connection between cults and child abuse,[7] there is almost no *scientific literature* available on the topic of child abuse in cults, despite a string of disturbing cases. Official investigations cover only a handful of extreme cases in which the death of a child served as a stimulus to government action.

What is certain, however, is the fact that child-rearing in a cult environment represents a radical departure from the general methods and standards of most Western societies. To what degree the issue of neglect or abuse is sustainable is irrelevant to the fact that children in cults are part of a system which is isolated from the mainstream. Although this may not be a geographical separation, from an ideological and philosophical view, cults are definitely isolationist in nature.

Children are often the first victims of relationship breakdowns resulting from cult experiences. Invariably, many of these matters end up in court. There is an urgent need within the judicial system for the courts to recognise the nature of mind control and the fact that a child's testimony regarding a preferred parent may be influenced by cult involvement. Failure to recognise these issues leaves open the possibility that the courts will deal inappropriately with children who are cult victims, thereby prolonging the destructive influence of many of these groups.

CASE STUDY: THE BIZARRE CULT OF THE BLEACH BLOND KIDS

'In an old holiday house on the shores of Lake Eildon they had been kept in isolation from the world, a wretched bunch of young people who had known no other life than ill-treatment at the hands of the woman and her followers who called themselves The Family. They had been starved of food and love and had suffered severe physical punishments.

'... our heads would be held under water until we almost drowned and we were made to watch our "sisters and brothers" being beaten. If one of us didn't own up to doing something wrong, we all paid the price ... There was no time to play and no life outside Eildon because we were never given enough food — sometimes as a punishment we would be left hungry for three days — we stole from the kitchen and buried our food under bush leaves. Later, when we thought it was safe, we would forage like animals to find it.'[8]

The Anne Hamilton-Byrne sect came to light in 1983, after a series of articles in *The Age* detailed the control that the sect leader, Anne Hamilton-Byrne, had over her followers. It was alleged that she used massive doses of the hallucinogenic drug LSD in houses in the Dandenongs and at a private psychiatric hospital run by medical professionals in her sphere of influence.

Already in 1980, an officer of the Education Department had given Anne Hamilton-Byrne's school its annual approval, despite the fact that he was uneasy about the regimentation of the fourteen children from the ages of five to fourteen — the way they were lined up and, like the Von Trapp family in *The Sound of Music*, gave their full names and dates of birth.

Another bizarre allegation relates to Anne Hamilton-Byrne's use of the Newhaven Private Hospital in Kew as a recruiting ground in the late 1960s. Even more disturbing was the use of the drug LSD by psychiatrists at the hospital. In her book *Unseen, Unheard, Unknown*,[9] Sarah Hamilton-Byrne, a former member of the group, claims that the psychiatrists would put members under the influence of LSD for days, even up to a week. These experiences were called 'go-throughs' or 'clearings'. One former patient who went public in a lengthy article[10] said that he first met Anne Hamilton-Byrne, who was then known as Mrs Riley, at the Newhaven Hospital. 'Mrs Riley became friendly with me — even then she had a sort of charisma. She suggested to me that on my discharge, it would be courting disaster to return to my bachelor flat in South Yarra and a better idea would be to come to stay with her ... it was not long before I was introduced to the mysteries of the procedures of the cult.'

The former patient was initiated into the sect and married another member at the suggestion of Anne Hamilton-Byrne. His marriage broke down and, at the time of his newspaper interview, he had not seen his children for four years. He detailed the clearings and named three psychiatrists who had been involved in administering the drugs.

Another woman said in a statutory declaration that she had attended the clearings, which were carried out six at a time at the hospital and at private residences. It was her duty to sit with the members while they were under the influence of drugs and report back to Anne Hamilton-Byrne, who then used this information to create the impression that she had psychic powers.

The purpose of the clearings was to assist members to come to terms with their past lives. They were told that if they didn't follow their leader, they would be destined for further reincarnation.

Anne Hamilton-Byrne's 'spiritual path' included regular beatings, verbal and emotional intimidation, food deprivation and the regular administration of drugs. 'For most of my early childhood, I was constantly hungry. We were starving and it was Anne's policy that we should remain so. We were so hungry we ate dirt and leaves. We were so hungry we ate grass and scavenged in the rubbish bins ... we were so hungry we stole anything we could. Vitamin C tablets were considered manna from Heaven.'[11]

One of the most baffling and disturbing aspects of the Anne Hamilton-Byrne case was the inaction on the part of the relevant government authorities. According to reports in *The Age* after it exposed the group in 1983, Victoria Police's Delta Taskforce into child exploitation recommended an investigation into the sect, but a senior officer ruled it unwarranted. *The Age* reports were brought to the attention of officers of Community Services Victoria. They took no action.

In response to questions in Parliament about the group in September 1983, the Education Minister undertook to have the school's file brought to him for assessment. *The Age* attempted to find out the results of the assessment, but the Directorate of School Education said that the 1983 file was missing.

A 1985 inspector's report of the 'school' accepted, as proof of contact with a wider society and awareness of the modern world, the children's ballroom dancing, trips to libraries, an interest in pop music, fashion and grooming. According to Sarah Hamilton-Byrne, in the weeks before the inspector's visit, the sect went into a state of panic, desperate to find ways to create the image of a worldly school.

Little did the authorities know about what was really going on in the cult. They knew nothing of the food deprivation or the administration of drugs, which has been well documented since that time. 'We regularly received major tranquillisers such as Anatensol and Serepax. We were all given the benzodiazepines, Valium and Mogadon, on a daily basis ... The climax of each child's drug taking came in the cult experience known as "going through". During the process, also known as clearing, we were given LSD and a number of other hallucinogenic drugs. Going through was basically a sustained LSD trip. It was meant to "clear" our souls and take us to a higher plane of understanding.'[12]

Nevertheless, a further request to the then Foreign Minister, Mr Hayden, to look into the affairs of the sect in relation to the possibility of passport irregularities proved futile, as the passports were in order.

According to *The Age*, it took the escape of a former member of the group from the Eildon house in mid-1987 to stir the Community Policing Squad into action. Subsequently the police raided the house and released the remaining six children. Again investigations into the issue of adoptions, as well as the role of sect members, were hindered by the disappearance of relevant files.

In 1988, the Government ordered a new police and Department of Community Services inquiry into the sect. No action was taken. The following year, as a result of a fire, which police had linked to the sect, Operation Forest was set up to investigate any issues of criminality surrounding the imprisonment of the children. Under the relevant statute of limitations, the investigations into allegations of child abuse were no longer viable.

Despite a report to the Director of Public Prosecutions in 1991, which contained recommendations of several charges against Anne Hamilton-Byrne, 18 months later it was decided to proceed with the charges relating to the issue of false birth registrations.

To the disgust of former members and the utter disappointment of numerous workers involved in the case, not one adult has been charged for the ill-treatment of the children, despite three major investigations and despite former members' allegations of beatings and starvation.

In her book, *Unseen, Unheard, Unknown*, Sarah Hamilton-Byrne says that she does not blame the individual police officers involved. 'Although the justice system let us down, I have nothing but praise for the police who were involved in our case.'

Nevertheless, Sarah Hamilton-Byrne's response to the inaction of the justice system may serve as an inspiration for other former members of cults. 'It took a long period for some of us to accept that there was never going to be any form of retribution for all these years of abuse. But to get on with life, one has to accept that things are not always fair. I have chosen the path of not wasting energy on feelings of bitterness at the system or hatred towards Anne for what she and her minions have done to me. I prefer to forgive and forget. I know the greatest way I can be compensated for and triumph over my childhood is to succeed in what I am doing, to live life fully and to learn what it is to be happy.

'If I can do that, I will have won and the cult will have lost. If I can achieve happiness, I will have gained far more for myself than any court case or retribution could have given me. For I will have transcended the legacy of being a child of The Family. I will have transcended the legacy of being a Hamilton-Byrne.'[13]

CHAPTER 15

CULTS AND THE MENTALLY ILL

'Early last year David was hospitalised. He was diagnosed with schizophrenia. Our family spent many months grieving and coming to terms with David's illness. We were surprised when, nine months later, he had improved and was well enough to leave hospital. Several weeks ago, we received a letter from him telling us he had joined an Eastern group and would be leaving for India in a few days. He wrote that he had been told to cease taking his medication. We have tried to contact him without success. A boarder who was living with him believes he is already in India ...' [1]

The possibility of mentally disturbed people being attracted to cults represents a nightmare for families and friends. Like the child who has become ensnared in a cult, the mentally ill person is defenceless and powerless to resist the overwhelming pressure of the group.

Studies vary on the composition of cults membership of in so far as mental health issues are concerned, with most research suggesting that the incidence of mental health problems amongst cult recruits mirrors that of the general population.

Nevertheless, the issue of cults and mental health is significant as cults have the potential to become a haven for the mentally ill and the emotionally unstable. Mental health professionals as well as families who have had to deal with mentally disturbed individuals are aware of the fact that mental illness can be accompanied by illusions of a religious or spiritual nature. It is not unusual for schizophrenics to associate the hearing of voices with a holy calling or a special relationship with God. Society is all too familiar with acts of violence and other atrocities attributed to a calling or divine message.

Throughout the world the trend towards de-institutionalisation has led to the attempt on the part of mental health authorities to reintegrate numerous mental health sufferers into the community. Invariably, these changes have created a far greater level of exposure to the community. Considering the vulnerability of these individuals, the cults can be particularly dangerous.

In the attempts of these people to make sense of their shattered lives in a world of confusion, the attractiveness of a cult can be magnified. Where independent living can be a day-to-day struggle, the lure of accommodation, food and comfort can be most inviting. If, in addition, the cult is able to offer counselling and support, the picture is complete.

But there is a deeper attractiveness about cults for the mentally ill. What has been diagnosed earlier as a particular form of illness will be regarded as a blessing within the cult philosophy. A spiritual message or a calling from above which suggests a troubled mind will be considered by the cult as characteristic of a blessing or special power. For the mentally ill to be regarded as blessed rather than disturbed, holy rather than confused, is certainly a reason to consolidate a relationship with the cult.

Whilst there are those who argue that this environment may be more supportive than the alternative of roaming the streets without purpose, the reality is that such comforts are usually short-lived. Cults have nothing to gain from this person. His inability to raise funds, the potential of spreading the wrong message and the potential to turn off other members means that sooner rather than later the person will be thrown out from the movement. Documented accounts of ex-members who have suffered such treatment have included stories of being driven hundreds of kilometres during the dark of night to be left stranded without money or food.

It is outrageous that in the face of an obvious need for medical assistance, these cults are able to justify a claim to have superior methods by which to treat the illness. Essentially, valuable time is being lost in the rehabilitative process so that any resumption of treatment later on will require greater effort with possibly a less favourable prognosis. In addition, the rejection by the cult after the short-lived euphoria of finally finding a welcome setting serves to further complicate the predicament of the mentally ill.

The anguish of families whose loved ones have joined cults is exacerbated by their awareness of the mental health of the person. Most cults take an anti-medication stance and the denial of medication to the member can serve only to increase the family's anxiety. The problem is further magnified by the person's inaccessibility by family, medical practitioners or psychiatrists.

Although the insular nature of cults and the insistence that any psychological or emotional problems be dealt with 'in house' are potentially dangerous for any cult member, the situation of the mentally ill is even more serious. Some cults brand all form of psychological or psychiatric intervention as evil.

Noticeable in its vehement opposition to the psychiatric profession is the Church of Scientology. In 1996, the *Cult Observer* reported the appearance of four magazines in a glitzy, bizarrely illustrated series: *Psychiatry, Education's Ruin*; *Psychiatry: Victimising the Elderly*; *Psychiatry's Betrayal* (on 'creating racism') and 'Psychiatry's Rape' (on psychiatry and female patients).[2]

Furthermore, in its efforts to support a bill in the Florida legislature which would strip power from the child abuse investigators, a spokesperson for the Citizens Commission on Human Rights (a group allied with Scientology) said, 'No activity in modern American history is as reminiscent of the destructive and terrifying abuse of power of the psychiatrists in Nazi Germany as that of the psychiatrists and other mental health practitioners currently operating in the child protective system.'[3]

Whereas there may be avenues whereby parents are able to approach relevant statutory bodies to assess child exploitation or negligence, these avenues do not exist, as a rule, with adults. In serious situations there is the risk of suicide or other self-destructive behaviour over which the family has no control. There is also the possibility of individuals doing harm to others as a result of their illness. In that respect the desperation of families is paramount — without any simple solution.

The cult's mind-altering techniques, the reframing of values and redefinition of the world are themselves reason for grave concern. However, when these changes are superimposed onto a trouble mind or fragmented personality, the resulting picture can be one of tragedy and hopelessness.

David, referred to in the opening paragraph, did travel to India, where he remained in the group for just three weeks. Without medication he swung from one psychotic episode to the next. Eventually, he was thrown out and managed to find his way back to his family in Australia. He stayed with them for one night and left early the following morning.

David was missing for two weeks. Eventually the family received a call from a psychiatric hospital in Sydney, stating their son had been admitted. He had been found wandering the streets, telling everyone he met that he was the new guru of the cult.

Luckily, David was found alive and was able to be treated. For every person who does survive and is healed, there are many more who are not so fortunate. Frightened by the cult and tormented by its beliefs, these people taste reality very quickly, only to find they have burnt their bridges and have nowhere to go.

PART 4

MIND CONTROL AND EXIT COUNSELLING

- ● BUT WHAT IS MIND CONTROL?

- ● THE CHALLENGE OF EXIT COUNSELLING

- ● FAMILY DIVISION OVER EXIT COUNSELLING

On a personal level, discovering the cult scene was an odyssey, in many ways a journey into the unknown. Visiting the various groups and participating in their activities was often a bizarre experience.

The range of groups, the nature of their beliefs and their different practices never ceased to amaze me. I found it incredible that people could be attracted to so-called philosophies which preached death and suicide. I was fascinated by the contrasts between groups: on the one hand, some practised celibacy and restriction while, on the other hand, there were groups which encouraged promiscuity and free sex.

But these mysteries could not be compared to the elusive notion of mind control: the fact that many cult members seemed to be under a spell or in some sort of trance. This was not a trance which made them look like zombies: many cult members looked and seemed to behave very 'normally'. This was a far deeper phenomenon, which affected every aspect of their existence, be it emotional, psychological, spiritual or financial.

I met people brought up in traditional families who had thrown out their moral codes within days of joining a cult and were prepared to lie and fabricate their stories without hesitation. Relationships changed dramatically and, in some situations, were cast away. Loving parents became enemies as values were changed and reframed.

I recognised that in order to 'bring these people home' it would be necessary for both them and their families to understand the nature of mind control. I learnt that exit counselling was a process which reversed the mind control and psychological manipulation which had been practised on the innocent cult victim.

It was encouraging to know that there was a professional response to the unprofessional behaviour of cults. Exit counselling was a process which had been refined from the earlier practice of deprogramming, which had often involved the use of force in isolating a cult member from a group.[1]

I met exit counsellors who were eager to point out the development of an ethics code by which they were bound: no involuntary work, no substitution of the cults' ideology with that of the counsellor, involvement of the family and a carefully planned follow-up program.

Exit counselling has become the professional response to mind control. Under the right conditions and with the necessary preparation, it works. Fundamental to its success is an understanding of the nature of mind control.

CHAPTER 16

BUT WHAT IS MIND CONTROL?

The stories are all too familiar. Simone completed high school and went on to study Arts at university. She was majoring in psychology and literature and was involved in a steady relationship. During her last semester in the final year, she announced that she was putting both the course and the relationship on hold in order to travel to the US to participate in the activities of a New Age movement in California. Within three days she was on her way, her ticket being funded by a loan from an American member of the movement. At the time of writing, four years down the track, Simone has not returned; contact with her family has been reduced to two postcards a year and there is no return address or even phone contact.

William and Terry had been married for 18 years and had lived together for four years prior to their marriage. They had two young children. Their relationship was viewed by friends as ideal. He was the perfect, caring, loving father, who left work early in order to spend time with his children. When William joined a trekking movement, he had no idea that it was the creation of a former psychiatrist who had established a small community in the outback of Australia. The philosophy, an unusual blend of mysticism and rational emotive therapy ideas, had created a close knit 'family' which opposed marriage, relationships and any sexual contact unless sanctioned by the leader. William did not return home for just under a year. Although he kept in contact with his children, he had minimal contact with his wife. On his return he announced his desire to divorce. He was quite content with the fact that his wife would have custody of the children.

Not every cult experience is so dramatic; nevertheless, the similarities between the two cases are striking, suggesting that there a common process at work, regardless of the origin and nature of the group.

The notion of 'love bombing' and unconditional acceptance has already been mentioned as a powerful influence during the early stages of recruitment. This behaviour, which appeals to all of us, in particular the down-and-out or those who have just terminated a relationship, continues on as the member integrates into the cult, although the intensity of it may decrease. Interestingly, as the individual becomes more involved in the cult, s/he realises that everybody receives the same treatment and that everybody is told they are 'special'. Unfortunately, by that time this realisation, which to an outsider would be a cause for concern, is not questioned.

But is this enough? What else is happening? More specifically, what is mind control?

Basing himself on the works of Leon Festinger, a psychologist,[1] Steve Hassan, in his epic work, *Combatting Mind Control*,[2] identifies four components of mind control. Although the original work suggests three components, Hassan has added a fourth. They are: control of behaviour, control of thoughts, control of emotions and control of information.

'Behaviour control is the regulation of an individual's physical reality. It includes control of his environment — where he lives, what clothing he wears, what food he eats, how much sleep he gets — as well as the jobs, rituals and other actions he performs.'[3]

Fasting, strict diet, the wearing of particular clothes, as well as highly regulated timetables, contribute to the behaviour control, as the member finds that s/he has very little or no private time. A reward and punishment code further restricts individual freedom as compliance takes on new significance. The regulation of the member's personal budget means s/he no longer has control over her/his money, often having to resort to borrowing from the cult. These loans in turn create further dependence on and attachment to the cult.

'*Thought control* includes indoctrinating members so thoroughly that they internalize the group doctrine, incorporate a new language system, and use "thought-stopping techniques" to keep their mind centered. In order to be a good member, a person must learn to manipulate his thought processes.'[4]

Cult members are not allowed to think negatively about the cult. The cults create a range of 'thought-stopping' techniques, which become quite mechanical in the face of negative thoughts. Singing, chanting, speaking in tongues, humming, focusing on the guru are an almost automatic response to doubt, anxiety and stress.

Particular expressions, clichés, sentences which are made to appear spontaneous but are learned and practised are also vehicles for thought control. In the same way a new student looks forward to mastering the language of her/his course, so too does the cult member regard the mastering of the group's language as a goal.

'*Emotional control* attempts to manipulate and narrow the range of a person's feelings. Guilt and fear are necessary tools to keep people under control.'[5]

Hassan points out how cults create an enemy who is persecuting you. This enemy can take the form of authority, such as the FBI's involvement with the Branch Davidians at

Waco. Deprogrammers are also the enemy. Some groups go to extraordinary lengths in order to denigrate deprogrammers and the anti-cult organisations.

The creation of phobias or phobia indoctrination is a powerful technique of emotional control. For example, members are warned that if they leave the cult they will experience disaster, get killed in plane crashes or die prematurely.

One of my first clients was a woman who had been thrown out of a cult some eight years before she saw me. She had since married but was afraid of becoming pregnant as she had been told that her children would be stillborn. She eventually did become pregnant and miscarried after three months, with her doctor claiming that her deep-seated fears and constant anxiety contributed to the miscarriage.

The creation of phobias leads to severe panic attacks at the thought of leaving; hence the desire to avoid that option. Eventually, it does not matter whether the members 'can leave at any time' — the doors can be wide open. After her capture by the US police authorities, Patty Hearst found it difficult to come to terms with the fact that she had the freedom to escape from the Symbionese Liberation Army but had not taken up that option.

Information control refers to the cults' withholding of information which is not conducive to cult adherence, as well as the selective presentation of other forms of information to the membership.

Many groups deny their members access to television or other forms of the media. They may provide a buddy to ensure that there is some control when outside family members visit. If information is passed on during that time which contradicts the cult's ideology, every effort will be made to neutralise that effect. It is not uncommon for cults to screen both incoming and outgoing mail.

Damning media reports about the cult and its leadership are withheld. In the event of information leaking into the cult, there are damage control mechanisms to attack it. Invariably, the media is Satan's agent and the information which has been disseminated should be regarded as a test.

These forms of mind control are powerful. We need to understand how they act to change the personality of the member.

In his excellent introduction to *Recovery from Cults*,[6] Michael Langone provides a succinct account of the cult indoctrination process:

'Those who do make the commitment to join are rarely aware of the subtle techniques of persuasion and control shaping their behaviour, thoughts and feelings. The apparent loving unanimity of the group masks, and in some cases, bolsters, strict rules against private as well as public dissent. Examples of such personal attacks may be, "You're intellectualising" or "You're being divisive." Doubt and dissent are thus interpreted as symptoms of personal deficiency.

'Once the dominance of the group is established, once it is permanently "one-up", members slide down a spiral of increasing dependence on the group. They are often encouraged or ordered to live with other group members. People outside the group are viewed as spiritually, psychologically, politically, or socially inferior, or as impediments to the members' development. In order to "advance" at a satisfactory pace, members must avoid outsiders and spend long hours involved in various tasks or practices the leadership deems necessary.'

To ensure continuation of the group's rewards (praise, attention, promise of future benefits, social contact and so on) members must implicitly, if not explicitly, acknowledge the group's authority in defining what is real, good and true.

The group challenges and tests the members' subservience by establishing extremely high, if not impossible, expectations regarding activities (for example, fundraising quotas) and personal development. Because dissent, doubt and negativity are forbidden, members must project a facade of 'happiness and acceptance', while struggling to achieve the impossible. Those who fail to establish the requisite facade are attacked and punished.

'The result of this process, when carried to its conclusion, is a *pseudo-personality*, a state of dissociation in which members are "split" but not "multiple", in which they proclaim great happiness yet hide great suffering.'[7]

Suggesting a similar outcome of the cult process, Hassan refers to the notion of *dual identity*, suggesting that despite all of the forces of mind control, the essential identity of the member is never totally destroyed. Its presence and manifestation will depend on the level of indoctrination or psychological manipulation experienced. Families should not be misled by the apparent re-emergence of the old personality or a temporary return to the pre-cult presentation.

Robert Lifton refers to the dramatic change of identity as *doubling*, 'the formation of a second self which lives side by side with the former one, often for a considerable time'.[8]

An alternative way of assessing the manner in which cults actually change the behaviour of potential adherents is by examining a three-stage process by which the group gains control of the individual. These three stages have been referred to as *unfreezing*, *changing* and *refreezing*.

The three stages are discussed in a book by Edgar Schein called *Coercive Persuasion*.[9] The model is based on the 1940 works of Kurt Lewin.[10]

Schein describes *unfreezing* as breaking a person down, *changing* as the actual process of indoctrination and *refreezing* as the rebuilding of a new identity or the pseudo-personality referred to above.

The unfreezing process includes the use of hypnosis and the inducement of a trance state. Changes of diet, sleep deprivation, a new wardrobe, as well as the denial of access to the media and other external stimuli, are powerful agents of change. So too are negative comments about the member, the denigration of the member's earlier life and family connections, as well as comments about spiritual inadequacy.

Changing refers to the superimposition of a new identity. Hassan says that many of the techniques used in the freezing phase are acted out during this phase. These include hypnosis, repetition, monotony and rhythm in order to further cement the member to the new world order of the cult and to further reinforce the belief that inside it is good, outside it is bad. The pressure is on to drop one's past and create the new person with a new truth.

During this period there is an outright effort to implant the cult ideology onto the member's mind. There is intense one-on-one dialogue with earlier recruits (which further strengthens their commitment). Normal barriers of privacy are broken down, as the member must share innermost private beliefs and experiences with the group. The peer pressure to conform and join with others is overwhelming; individuality becomes lost in the totality of the group experience.

And finally the process of *refreezing* involves the creation of a new identity and new purpose. Externally, with the change of dress and name as well as the use of particular language, and internally, with subjugation to the leader and negation of previous relationships and life experience, the member establishes a new life.

The member is now allowed out to collect funds and to recruit others. Now trusted in both these areas the group responds by attaching a level of importance and stature to the member. The member knows, or at least is under the impression that s/he knows what is happening on the inside; yet the member withholds that information from new recruits in the same way it was withheld from them.

A final point in relation to the expression 'brainwashing'. Although some experts use the words 'brainwashing' and 'mind control' interchangeably[11] the majority of opinion favours a distinction between the two issues, suggesting that brainwashing refers to the product of coercion whereby the victim is aware of the process. As a result, examples of brainwashing include the Korean prisoners of war, the victims of Chinese thought reform or the American hostages held by Iran.[12]

But regardless of the definitions and the relevant terms, it is the disturbing result which counts, because, ultimately, the cult becomes the member's family and true purpose in life. The process is complete.

CHAPTER 17

THE CHALLENGE OF
EXIT COUNSELLING

'Exit counselling is not mysterious. At heart, it is simply respectful communication. In a way it is analogous to Radio Free Europe or the Voice of America transmitting information "through" the iron curtain to the people living in the closed societies of Eastern Europe and the former Soviet Union. There is no magic. There is merely the patient, persistent communication of that which ultimately shatters all walls: truth, honesty, respect and love.'[1]

Counselling involves a voluntary process whereby an individual or family seek assistance in relation to particular problems or issues relevant at the time. Marital counselling may focus on issues of balance or compatibility in a relationship. Drug and alcohol counselling may focus on the nature of addictions and the implications of extended use.

In all of these situations the counselling affects a specific area of the individual's life, which, in varying degrees, will affect other areas of the person's functioning, whether it be at home, in the context of a relationship, or in the workplace. Essentially, the individual's life is continuing, and counselling will hopefully resolve outstanding issues and improve the quality of life.

Most counsellors and therapists are reluctant to see clients who are unwilling to participate in the process. Many will insist that the client makes his/her own appointment as a condition for acceptance. Often the intensity of the therapy or the program will influence the level of motivation required. For example, people on waiting lists for long-term residential therapeutic programs are often required to telephone the program co-ordinators every day in order to remain on the list.

In stark contrast, in terms of the cult environment and experience as well as the issue of motivation, exit counselling stands apart from other more standard types of counselling and other forms of therapeutic intervention.

Exit counselling is the response to a process which has involved every area of the individual's experience and psyche. The intensity of the cult experience has had a massive impact on every issue of the individual's life, from a psychological, emotional and spiritual point of view. Family relationships have been altered, if not severed. The cult has reframed the member's view of life and the world.

Exit counselling does not focus on a particular aspect of the individual's functioning but on the entire existence and environment of the cult member and the dramatic ramifications of cult life. The nature of the environment in which the counselling is to take place, the ability of the counsellor to establish a relationship of trust and, most importantly, the counsellor's capacity to engage the client and hold her/his attention are all paramount factors in the success of the exit counselling process.

Furthermore, from the cult member's point of view, all forms of therapy have been branded as satanic and evil. Psychiatrists and psychologists are the weapons of Satan. If cult members require any form of assistance or counselling, it is done 'in-house'. Exit counsellors are viewed as kidnappers who charge exorbitant fees to destroy other people's lives. The cult members have been trained to resist any form of intervention at any cost. Organisations have produced their own manuals to assist in the indoctrination of the members regarding this issue.

To break this deadlock and re-establish communication with the cult member requires planning and foresight. It calls for an understanding of the particular cult, as well as an insight into the psyche of the cult member. Somebody, be it a relative or friend or someone who once knew the individual, will need to make the first move to re-open the lines of communication.

It may take weeks or months for the appropriate person to pave the way for this to take place and that person will require guidance and instruction every step of the way. There are no shortcuts or fast tracks. It is well established that families who have rushed in to save a loved one have had minimal, if any, success.

One of the first questions I ask the family during my initial contact relates to the possible involvement of a sibling, relative or friend who may be able to assist. I refer to this person as a facilitator. Interestingly, although initially families find it difficult to think of anyone, on further consideration this changes as they consider the member's early friendships and relationships. In my work with cult members I have successfully resorted to a range of people to assist. They have included former boyfriends and girlfriends, former classmates, teachers and members of the clergy.

If successful, the facilitator will be able to convince the cult member of the value of meeting with a third person for any of a number of reasons. For example, 'Your parents are really falling apart, and though you are no longer close to them, I find it hard to see this happening ... I've met the person, he's great, you can't lose by meeting him ... I've been thinking about you and

I want you to know that I'm concerned; can we talk together and maybe even with someone else?... I'll be there with you.'

The use of a facilitator works best in situations where the cult member is experiencing inner conflict or genuine doubt. This may be the result of a close friend leaving or the fact that another prophecy has failed to materialise. Other triggers which may assist the facilitator in achieving their aim include negative publicity, which the cult member may have seen, or the imposition of a schedule — fundraising or witnessing — which has been too taxing.

A sense of loneliness in the cult despite the charade of friendship and support, the absence of any contact with the opposite sex or the fear of being married off to a stranger are all factors which can provide the incentive for a relationship with an outsider.

The facilitator will be instructed in how to sense these weaknesses and how to find an appropriate time for a meeting. The timing is important in that it will be difficult to suggest an outside meeting if, for example, the cult is celebrating a major event, or if a new group of recruits is being inducted. Conversely, it may be easier to engage the member if the cult has been receiving negative publicity, if a group of people have left or if the numbers are down.

The involvement of an untrained or inexperienced facilitator often puts that person into a position of onerous responsibility. It is therefore imperative that throughout this process, the facilitator receives assistance and adequate support and is not put under any pressure which may translate into a sense of guilt and inadequacy if the process is unsuccessful.

Although I am generally optimistic about the use of a facilitator, there will be situations where, despite every effort and good intention, the cult member will not attend a meeting. This may be a consequence of the level of detachment from their family, refusing to have any association whatsoever, or of the fear the cult has implanted in the member in relation to contact with outsiders.

Alternatively, the member may agree to a meeting on the cult premises, or a meeting conditional on another cult member being present. They may even agree to meet the family on its own 'home ground' but stipulate that the meeting be no more than an hour.

The alternative then becomes what Hassan refers to as a covert intervention, which involves a level of deception. Hassan states his discomfort with the notion of any form of deception, as this is one of the very issues for which the cults can be condemned, but he does make the point that, unlike the case of the cults, this approach is not aimed at creating any form of allegiance to a leader or group. 'Once my job of presenting information ... and counselling is accomplished, it is up to the individual to make use of the experience.'[2]

Essentially, a covert intervention involves the engagement of a cult member for reasons other than exit counselling. Various strategies can be employed in the event of a covert intervention being necessary. The decision to attempt this approach ultimately depends on the severity of the situation, as well as any risks surrounding ongoing involvement in the group.

Although all interventions require careful preparation, a covert intervention must be handled with extra care. The family needs to recognise that a failed attempt to assist their loved one may be met with a very negative response, possibly the severing of the relationship entirely.

An intervention presents the family with an opportunity, and the chances of being successful depend on a positive attitude. Indeed, exit counselling presents the family with an enormous challenge. The way in which this challenge is accepted can have a significant bearing on the outcome.

CHAPTER 18

FAMILY DIVISION OVER EXIT COUNSELLING

I recall counselling a family in relation to their daughter, who had become involved in the Children of God. On one of my visits I noted the growing pile of papers, faxes and e-mails relating to the case. They were all placed in a very noticeable position on the parents' study desk. When questioned as to why these documents were being displayed so prominently, the father responded he wanted to ensure that in the event of his daughter coming home voluntarily or being thrown out of the cult, he would be able to show the effort that had been made by the family to bring her home.

Although the development and refinement of the exit counselling process has enhanced the possibility of a loved one leaving a cult, the issue nevertheless remains controversial.

Apart from the controversy that continues in the broader community, there is also the possibility that the family will be divided over the question of involvement.

There are numerous issues to consider. One central issue remains the right to interfere with the so-called decision of an adult who has chosen to participate in a cult organisation's activities. Despite all the academic arguments regarding free choice, coercion and informed decisions, families still find it difficult to come to terms with the concept of intervention. With all the assurances regarding the sensitivities of exit counselling and the professional nature of the process, there is still hesitation.

My experience has shown that this resistance is based, amongst other things, on ignorance and the lack of a comprehensive understanding of the cult's operations. The processes of psychological manipulation are very subtle, and it is not difficult to push them aside when it comes to deciding whether to go ahead with an intervention. As well as denial, families can move towards a 'wait-and-see' position, rather than go ahead with anything else.

The other significant issue is the fear of alienation from the cult member if the exit counselling is unsuccessful. It is impossible to totally dismiss this concern although, if the counselling is carried out properly, the chances of it happening are very low. Professional exit counsellors, as compared with the earlier deprogrammers, are able to put in place a range of safeguards for the family relationship if the counselling is unsuccessful. These safeguards can be considered an eject hatch in the face of imminent danger, where it appears that there will be no resolution of the problem.

The issue of guilt arising over inaction is also a relevant factor. Parents may be concerned about the reaction of their loved one if they emerge from the cult years later to find that the prime of their life has been lost. The thought that the potential college years are passing by, that the opportunity for relationships and possibly children is diminishing only adds to the forces of guilt pushing the parents towards a more pro-active position.

As strong as these feelings may be, they cannot be the only reason for proceeding with an intervention. This enormous task requires positive motivation and plenty of enthusiasm.

It is not always possible to reach a unanimous decision backed by all members of the family. Where there is a direct conflict of opinion, counselling cannot proceed; there must be a resolution. A resolution does not mean total agreement; it does mean that there is an understanding that some family members may choose not to be involved whilst agreeing that other members will have to carry this on their own. Although not an ideal situation, it is certainly workable. Hopefully, in that situation, those family members who are not involved will still be in a position to lend their support to the intervention once the decision has been made to go ahead. An example of support may involve looking after children or minding the house.

It is wrong to attempt to influence a family in relation to its decision to go ahead or not with any form of intervention. Ironically, and in contrast to the cults, they need to make an informed decision without pressure or stress. The orientation meeting will have provided the basis for this assessment. Hopefully, the information provided will have been supplemented by reading and further research.

I suggest to families that they ask themselves a series of questions and actually discuss the answers as a means to making the right decision. Do they understand the concept of psychological manipulation? Do they understand the nature of mind control? Are they aware of the long-term implications of belonging to a cult?

I suggest the family members examine whether they really understand the nature of exit counselling and their part in it. Do they appreciate the voluntary nature of the process? Are they aware of the steps that will be taken to avoid alienation in the event of the process not being as successful as they would have liked?

The family needs to understand that it too must explore the possibility of change if there is to be any expectation of change on the part of their loved one. The involvement of family must be backed up by a readiness to change where necessary to accommodate the realities of the situation.

I recall a situation involving a divorced couple's son who had joined an obscure mystical sect in India. An unfortunate feature of the family life was the fact that since the divorce, when the boy was nine years old, the parents had never spoken. Any joint issues had been handled by a third person. For eleven years this young man had never seen his parents in the same room. Their decision to travel together to India and to meet with their son proved justified. Despite his deep involvement with the group — he was about to be married to one of its leaders — he agreed to meet with an exit counsellor in response to his parents' efforts. Eventually, he left the group and returned home with his parents.

And finally, for an intervention to go ahead there must be solid trust between the family and the exit counsellors, an understanding and open relationship which allows for discussion and disagreement where necessary. As much as time is always a factor, there is no way in which one can fast track this process, especially in relation to the issue of relationship building and trust.

The family needs to understand the notion of aftercare and the changes it may require. This issue is dealt with in a later chapter. Costs are always an issue and, although it is not always possible to predict them accurately, a good assessment of what is involved is certainly possible.

It is fascinating to see how resolving these dilemmas can be a very therapeutic exercise for the family. Negative behavioural traits displayed during the family meetings provide insights into the family dynamics, which can help explain the cult involvement of a loved one. I recall a family meeting which was chaired by the father of the boy involved. It looked more like a business conference than a family meeting. The father's authoritarian approach, his meticulous preparation, as well as the distribution of tasks to the other family members was, on one hand, impressive. On the other, it was overbearing and invasive and a possible explanation for why their son had left home to join a breakaway sect of the Family of Love.

My own experiences back up a sentiment that has been mentioned by many exit counsellors and professionals working in the field; it is that, regardless of the outcome, the exit counselling process is bound to create long-term positive change within the dynamics of the family. Even if the intervention does not go ahead, the process by which it has been discussed and resolved can be worthwhile.

PART 5

WHAT SHOULD WE DO NOW?

- We Are So Concerned — What Should We Do?

- Co-operation and Confidentiality

- What Are Our Choices?

- The Orientation Meeting

Inquiries about cults come from every sector of society. At Cult Counselling Australia, we receive calls from parents and families, community leaders, private practitioners and the police. Cults have been an issue in the home and the school, in the courts and in parliament, amongst community groups and in the media.

It is difficult for parents to come to terms with the fact that their loved one has joined a cult. As parents we all experience the challenge of our children growing up and becoming young adults. The control we are able to exercise over our children is diminished as they mature. If this move towards independence is thwarted by the control of a cult group, it is understandable that parents become very frustrated. When their loved ones turn against them, the frustration turns to anger. However, the situation becomes dangerous if the anger is directed at the cult member. 'Why in hell did you join?... I can't believe that you let us down ... You're going to have to make up for what you have done ...' These sentiments are inappropriate.

I have had to convince a very angry father that he had no right to punish his son for joining a cult. I have confronted a very emotional mother who suggested that in view of the hardship her daughter had caused her family, maybe the cult was the best punishment.

Perhaps the most common question parents ask is, 'What should we do now?' And perhaps the most relevant response is, 'Don't be angry with your child, don't reprimand them or give them a hard time'.

People do not join cults of their own volition. The fact that a loved one has become involved is not their fault; they can't be blamed. It is equally counter-productive for parents to blame themselves and begin to ask the age-old question, 'Where did we go wrong? He had such a happy childhood ... '

When it comes to helping a loved one leave a cult, the worst thing parents can do is play the 'blame game'. The best thing they can do is strengthen the lines of communication and do everything possible to retain an open relationship with their loved one.

From there onwards it becomes a question of finding the best avenue for professional help. Cult problems don't just go away like the common cold or a headache. In fact, over time they can become worse. For many, it is difficult to seek help; it is, however, a step which very few people ever regret.

CHAPTER 19

WE ARE SO CONCERNED — WHAT SHOULD WE DO?

'We think Jodie is involved in a cult ... Leah has really changed over the past few months ... Steven was never interested in religion until now ... Karen has just dropped her friends ... Alan won't talk to us about the group ... Dion is just not the same person ... We are so concerned — what should we do?'

If you have been reading this book in order of chapters, you will now know that cults are a complex issue, that there are many types of cults and that involvement with a group does not necessarily mean the same thing for everyone. As with any social ill, different people require different responses, and it is important for families to be directed towards the most appropriate means of assistance.

There are several things which parents can and should do as part of their initial response to a perceived problem related to a cult experience. I find it useful to present concerned families with a set of criteria to measure the involvement of a loved one in a cult. Although it may be difficult to respond to each item on the list, if the majority of the questions are answered in the affirmative, the family will have reason to be concerned and will have to decide how to deal with the situation.

- Is the person spending increasing time with the group?
- Is the person spending less time with parents, partner or other people they are generally close to?
- Are these relationships becoming more superficial?
- Is the person showing decreased interest in his earlier religious practice?
- Is her/his present religious or spiritual practice out of context?
- Has the person lost her/his sense of humour?
- Has the person experienced any recent trauma or hardship?
- Has she/he become less tolerant to society as a whole?
- Have there been any noticeable changes in regard to hobbies and personal interests?
- Has the person lost interest in politics, in reading the newspaper?
- Are there noticeable differences in the person's financial requirements?

Families should also attempt to find out all they can about the group which is causing concern. They may be able to write directly to the group and request information, although it is preferable to ask a friend do this. Cults may become very suspicious when the family of a member seeks information. The Internet and cult information centres are other avenues for information. Newspapers, the media in general and press clipping services can be useful.

It is also helpful to read books about the nature of cults, although at this stage, before any decisions have been made, it is unnecessary to 'read every book on the market'.

During this soul-searching time, families are often at a loss as to how they should relate to their loved one. Although the following suggestions may sound simplistic, they are vital.

Firstly, do not condemn or judge the group outright. Unless you feel that the person involved would welcome your opinion or ideas, it is preferable not to force a confrontation. There is no value in arguing rationally with a person who is a victim of mind control. Any reservations you express must be accompanied by a positive reinforcement of your love and concern for the person. Approval of particular aspects of the cult ideology, such as abstinence from drugs or promiscuity, should not be misconstrued as blanket approval of the organisation.

Secondly, try to find ways of bonding with your loved one and spending times together. Don't be afraid of talking about any problems or personal issues you may be experiencing. This may facilitate a response and an opportunity for improved communication.

Thirdly, parents may attend a church service or meditation session. This will show that you have an open mind and are willing to listen and learn. However, it is important to give the cult member opportunities to defend her/himself rather than enter into situations where they can defer to one of the cult authorities for the correct answers. A word of caution: I discourage siblings or even friends from participating in any cult-like activities, for fear of their becoming involved.

Fourthly, keep a diary of your loved one's involvement, so that you become aware of any changes. If the person is living with you, your regular contact may prevent you from noticing the changes that are taking place. The diary will be very useful when you do see a counsellor regarding your concerns.

All of the above information about the family member as well as your responses and behaviour will become important in deciding whether you take the matter any further and, if so, what path to take.

And lastly, don't send money. The chances are that it will simply be transferred to the group. I recall a situation where a young girl in the Moonies was receiving an allowance of $100 per week from her parents. This continued for seven years. After she was successfully counselled, she admitted to her parents that every cent they had provided had gone to help her reach her fundraising quota. If the member requires clothes or toiletries, you buy them and deliver them. It also gives you a little more input into what is being bought or how the money is being spent.

Inevitably, families will feel guilty about the fact that their loved ones have joined a cult. In some way or another, it is viewed as a reflection on their parenting or family values. Parents begin to become excessively introspective about the past, the time they have spent with their children, their education and their social scene. Whilst there may be lessons to be learnt, mind control has become a fact of life, and apportioning blame or feeling guilty is simply out of place.

Feelings of guilt or shame can lead to the dangerous tendency to overreact by intimidating the cult member and denigrating the group. These feelings are the very sentiments on which the cults capitalise in their efforts to display the disparity between the spirit of harmony and acceptance in the group and the conflict and confrontation at home.

Finally, it is common during these times for families to neglect their own needs. Although the person may have been involved in the organisation for a long time, there is a tendency to suddenly treat the situation as a matter of extreme urgency. Family routines are upset, commitments are put on hold and stress levels rise. It is important for the family to understand that life must go on. Any stress levels generated by the cult involvement may affect the family's level of communication with their loved one, as well as hindering its ability to work towards a viable plan and solution.

CHAPTER 20

CO-OPERATION AND CONFIDENTIALITY

Several years ago, I was approached by a family whose son had joined a psycho-therapeutic cult. The family had difficulty in understanding the gravity of the situation, and I had reservations about taking on the case. There was also a language barrier, which called for the use of an interpreter. The family was determined to press ahead, and I worked with them for several weeks in preparation for an intervention. The plan was to bring out two American exit counsellors. Considering the distance to Australia, the cost of the intervention was going to be considerable, but the family agreed.

Two days before the scheduled intervention, the parents called me to cancel the arrangement and to apologise for having taken the matter into their own hands. Their son had left for overseas. Apparently under pressure from relatives who had no idea of what cults were all about, the parents had called their son to a meeting. They had told him that it was time for them to be honest and admit that they had organised an intervention to remove him from the group. It was going to be expensive so, 'Why can't you just leave the group and we'll give you the money we would have spent on the intervention?' The boy agreed and accepted the money. He also bought a ticket the next day to join an overseas branch of the group. He did not leave an address.

As soon as the family decides that they would like to explore their options, the issue of confidentiality becomes paramount. Cults are very capable of moving members around, even sending them overseas without notice. Cult members are taught to look out for any signs of a possible intervention.

In the 1992 raids on the Children of God, one of the Community Services Victoria witnesses said that at the end of the children's beds were suitcases known as 'flee bags'. The witness said that she had been told the group could move at two hours' notice if members were followed or if people were asking questions.[1]

Breaches of confidentiality may be very subtle or quite blatant. I recall having to withdraw from an intervention at the last minute. The case related to a woman involved with the Rajneesh group; during the week she lived at the Rajneesh ashram and on weekends she came home. A few days before the planned intervention, her husband called from interstate asking her to take his suit to the dry cleaner. She cleaned out the pockets, only to find her husband's notes from a previous meeting with one of the exit counsellors.

From the very beginning, the only people who can be involved must be trustworthy and capable of remaining silent. Rather than involve many people and then reduce the group as the family moves towards the intervention, it is preferable to start with a very small group and then expand it if necessary. It is sometimes necessary to forego the participation and input of a family member or friend because of a concern about confidentiality.

As we have said, siblings are often well suited to encourage the cult member to meet the exit counsellors. Friends can also be a valuable channel of communication with the cult victim. However, they need to understand that involvement requires learning and education. It may be difficult to maintain ongoing contact with the cult member whilst, at the same time, making an effort to find out about the group, study the issue of cultism and be involved in preparations for the intervention.

On a more practical level, there are several steps families can take to ensure that there are no breaches of confidentiality.

Do not leave any books, including this one, around the house. All files and records must be stored out of reach and in safekeeping. All calls between the family and exit counsellor should be made from another location — not the family home — and in privacy. There should be no possibility of eavesdropping by the cult member. There are particular situations where I recommend that phone calls be made from public phone booths if there is reason to believe that the home phone is bugged. I do not recommend the use of mobile phones at any time, as crossed lines are not uncommon.

Any mail between the exit counsellor and the family should be directed to a post-box, preferably used for this purpose only. The use of e-mail and the Internet must be discreet. All files which have been opened for the purpose of research must be deleted.

Once the family becomes involved with a counsellor or agency, it is vital that every step of the way is negotiated together. Interventions have failed because family members took matters into their own hands and did not work as a team.

If the family is unhappy about any aspect of the plan, they should discuss it with the counsellor. Interventions are difficult and stressful. Small cracks in the relationship of the exit counsellor and the family have the potential of becoming gaping holes under the pressure of an argument or disagreement.

Confidentiality becomes particularly relevant as a result of a recent disturbing development: the decision of some groups to join together for the purpose of silencing their critics. Groups which have no association with each other have used each other's resources to attack exit counsellors and the anti-cult movement. Picking up on a phone conversation or an intercepted letter, these groups have attempted to involve the police and the law. Because, as a rule, exit counsellors are not in breach of the law, this activity amounts to little more than grandstanding. The involvement of the police and the law is usually a futile exercise at the taxpayers' expense.

However, such efforts by the cults can create frustration and anxiety for the families seeking assistance. Confidentiality is one means by which these attacks can be thwarted, so that whatever strategy is formulated can be implemented.

Families often find it hard to work in such secrecy. They feel that they are being as deceptive as the cults. Telling them that the end justifies the means seems too close to the practices they have condemned. They need to understand the difference between the cult experience and the issue of confidentiality which underlies the preparation for an intervention.

A few comments are relevant here. In the intervention, as soon as the meetings with exit counsellors have begun, there is full disclosure regarding the purpose of the meeting. The first contact with the cult member is open and honest. The cult member is informed that the family has organised the meetings so that together they can explore the information being presented, as well as the options of remaining with the group or leaving. The exit counsellors will identify themselves and explain what they intend to do.

The cults, on the other hand, are not honest at the first encounter with the potential recruit. They may not say who they are or the name of the group they represent. It may take weeks to find out. The practices and beliefs of the cult are never spelt out at the first meeting, and there is no disclosure about the long-term agenda of the group.

Cults usually promote a one-way flow of information. Exit counselling is a two-way process. Cults create psychological and emotional barriers in order to prevent a person from leaving. Exit counsellors are trained to share information, not emotions. Cults aim to keep the recruit for as long as possible. Exit counsellors would like to see their task as very short term.

And finally, former members have no problems with the confidentiality which surrounded the preparation for the intervention. Invariably, they understand that if the cult had been made aware of the plans, the intervention would not have gone ahead. The former members also know that had the cult not practised its perverse form of secrecy, they would never have joined in the first place.

CHAPTER 21

WHAT ARE OUR CHOICES?

'She's still part of our family and always will be. That will never change. The pain is always there. Birthdays and Christmas are always hard. I called her on her birthday this year and she called her grandmother and me on our birthdays. That's the first time she's done that for years. I was surprised. Moved. Emotional. And hopeful. Always hopeful that one day I'll get my daughter back.' [1]

The most effective way of looking at your choices is to discuss the situation with a counsellor who understands the cult scene. This discussion should not be regarded as a commitment in any direction but rather an opportunity to assess the situation and to explore the various options. I refer to this first encounter as an *orientation meeting*.

I conduct these meetings very regularly and find that my ability to assist the family is enhanced by covering a number of specific themes.

Prior to the orientation meeting, the intending participants are required to fill out a detailed form. The form covers basic information about the family background: parents' names, siblings, dates of births, occupations, employment, etc. It also requests information on the individual about whom the family is concerned. This includes educational background as well as interests and hobbies. Questions are asked about the particular cult, when the person joined, and whether it is a residential setting. There is a request for references and permission to follow them up if required.

The form provides an opportunity to assess whether the inquiries are genuine. The most common alternative is an inquiry emanating from a cult which is keen to find out what we do. On several occasions we have engaged in lengthy preliminary discussions only to find that the interested party will not fill out the form. It has left us wondering about the origin of the inquiry.

Once the form has been filled out satisfactorily, the orientation meeting can go ahead. It can last anything from two or three hours up to a full day. My agenda includes the following:

- An understanding of the family background.
- A profile of the person the family is concerned about.
- A detailed review of the cult phenomenon.
- The options the family may want to consider, including an intervention.
- Practical issues, such as choice of counsellor, timing, venue and costs.
- Goal clarification.
- Guarantees and definitions of success.

The orientation meeting is discussed in detail in the following chapter. If my assessment is that there is a problem which may be resolved through a form of intervention, I suggest that the family consider this option and let me know what their intentions are. It is important for the family to take the necessary time to consider their options.

There may be genuine reasons for not proceeding: lack of consensus on the issue, the presence of another family crisis which would affect the ability to be fully committed to the intervention, the cost factor or the non-availability of appropriate exit counsellors.

Two other factors should be incorporated into the decision-making process. Many people do leave cults and the fact that most people leave eventually has been used to show that the control cult leaders exercise is not absolute.[2]

One possibility is that members leave of their own accord. This may be the result of disillusionment or a personal crisis. Kathy was 23 years old when she joined an obscure Indian cult in northern Australia. Following a two-year initiation period, she was introduced to her partner and was married one week later. A day after the wedding, Kathy's partner informed her that he was bi-sexual and had been involved sexually with the leader of the movement. Furthermore, that relationship would have to continue if the leader requested it. Kathy packed her bags and left that same day.

Members may also leave of their own accord because the leader's deception is becoming so obvious that there is little room for ongoing allegiance and devotion — for example, when the world doesn't end, yet again.

The other possibility is that a member will be thrown out of a cult. If the member's behaviour becomes too embarrassing for the group or if they are a financial burden, the cult may simply request them to leave or forcibly remove them. This issue has already received attention in an earlier chapter in relation to cult members suffering from a mental health problem.

There have been occasions when a member was thrown out of a cult because of the pressure the family was putting on the group, either through personal approaches or through the media. Cults do not like negative publicity and are quite vulnerable to outside pressure. If the cult feels that the benefit of retaining the member is outweighed by the negative public exposure, it is very possible the member will be asked to leave. Nevertheless, families must appreciate that the use of outside forces or the media can be counter-productive; there is the possibility the member will be transferred interstate or even overseas.

I strongly advise families not to rely on their member either leaving or being thrown out. It is equally important to point out that most people who have left a cult of their own accord or have been thrown out may still require extensive counselling and time for recovery. In the latter case, the trauma associated with being thrown out can be very severe, since the former member is denounced and intimidated. He or she may be included on a hate list and forbidden to have contact with the group.

Furthermore, even if there are reasonable prospects that the member may leave, there are still arguments in favour of some form of intervention. Firstly, the longer the member remains with the group, the greater the potential for damage and the lengthier the recovery period required. Secondly, the fact that the family was involved in assisting the member to leave is a positive contribution, which can lead to an easier rebuilding of relationships after the cult experience. It would be understandable for former cult members to question the inaction of parents aware of the destructive nature of the cult.

The ability and desire of the family to go ahead with intervention, the fact that the member may leave of his/her own accord or be thrown out — all these possibilities must be thoroughly canvassed. If the family does decide to proceed, it is imperative they begin to familiarise themselves with what lies ahead, the challenges, the dilemmas and the responsibilities. These issues form the basis of the orientation meeting, which is discussed in the following chapter.

And if they decide not to proceed, there are numerous options which they must assess to maintain communication by transmitting the right messages to their loved one while, at the same time, leaving open the possibility of some intervention at a later date. These options are also discussed later.

CHAPTER 22

THE ORIENTATION MEETING

'In my years of working with ex-cultists and their families, I have seen one common problem that keeps tripping them up — they don't study mind control techniques properly. They read articles and books and watch videos, but do not really study and work the materials as if their life depended on it, yet it does . . .

'Parents want to get their child out of the clutches of the cult, assuming everything can then get back to normal. Once out, the problem is solved. Right? Wrong! Remember, intervention is only the beginning of the recovery process. The more the ex-cultist and the family do their homework, the faster and more thorough the recovery can be.'[1]

The orientation meeting represents the first formal contact between the counsellor/s and the family. Although there will have been telephone contact and the exchange of information about the case, this is the first opportunity for the counsellor/s and the family to work through an agenda.

The issue of confidentiality has already been addressed. It is imperative that those who participate in the meeting are aware of the need to keep it totally confidential. Regardless of the potential input of a family member or friend, there is no room for compromise. The meeting should be organised at a venue which leaves no possibility of it being visited by the person the family is concerned about. Similarly, it is important that no literature or documents are left behind which could create a confidentiality breach.

THE FAMILY BACKGROUND

My first objective is to gain an understanding of the family background. The information I seek relates to the number of children, their ages, their educational background and their plans for the future, if appropriate. I am interested in the children's relationships with their parents, whether, for example, there is a preference for father or mother.

Has the family been through any trauma — marital problems, divorce, a car accident, loss of a close relative or child, unemployment and financial difficulty, a court case? Is the family religious in nature, does God or religious service form part of the family life? Is there any evidence of a 'favourite' child? Have any other members of the family been involved in a cult or spiritual group?

The answers to these and many more questions can provide vital clues about the background to and the reasons for the cult involvement. For example, I have found a disproportionate number of members whose parents are divorced. Tragedy in a family may set off a pattern of soul-searching. Times of political unrest based on religious convictions may serve to enhance the appeal of cults that preach brotherhood and equality.

THE CULT VICTIM — A PERSONALITY PROFILE

It is not an easy task to draw up a profile of the cult victim. Nevertheless, without it, it is not possible to create a relevant and viable plan.

Once again, there are numerous aspects of the cult victim's personality and character that are important. The issue of self-esteem is one such example, the way the individual feels about him/herself includes everything from how comfortable they are with their body image to the ability to attract friends and remain socially active.

Of particular interest is any prior involvement with religion or any form of ideological practice. The relationship of the person with the family and parents and the way the person believes they are regarded is important. Issues of privacy and secrecy are also valuable: do they confide in anyone? Who? How often? Do they keep a diary?

Issues of dependence and neediness are important. How emotional is the person? Are they naive and gullible? How capable is the person of expressing themself? Do they find it easy to form relationships — short-term and long-term?

This information assists in understanding how the cult appears to have filled the person's needs. Is it because the person is looking for a father figure, or is it because the family religion is too abstract? Does the person feel a need to be loved and accepted? Have they just been through a personal crisis, or is life becoming too demanding? Are the cult's 'simple solutions to complex problems' looking too attractive?

Is there a history of mental health problems either with the cult victim or with the family? Is the cult victim on any medication? These are particularly important issues that, depending on the severity of the issue, may require a psychiatric opinion before one can proceed further.

Do the cult members feel that their identity problems and possible uncertainty about their sexuality are forcing them out of their family and circle of friends? Is the sexual abstinence preached by the group a convenient way of avoiding these issues? Or do they feel that the group may help them 'come out' and avoid the family pressures that surround them?

Is it the closeness of the group dynamics that attracts the person? Does that contrast with the more removed and distant attitude of their family or, for that matter, of their partner?

A REVIEW OF THE CULT PHENOMENA

During this part of the meeting, I attempt to provide an overview of cultism. I assume that the family has read the recommended literature prior to the meeting. I have found that the presentation of a number of case histories as well as the use of videos can help consolidate the family's understanding of cultism. In particular, the videos *Thy Will Be Done* and *The Wave* project a powerful message about mind control.

Following the overview, I put the particular group that the family is concerned about under the microscope in order to verify that it is a cult and that it has the potential to hurt the person involved. The family may have picked up material from overseas sources or from the Internet. It is important for families to understand that the particular practices of a cult in one part of the world may not be replicated in another part. It is also important that they appreciate the different levels of cult involvement. Two people may be involved in the same group with very different degrees of commitment and hence be exposed to different levels of risk.

The orientation meeting is an opportunity for the family to come to grips with the subtleties and complexities of cultism and dispel some of the incorrect images projected by the media. Although, as mentioned earlier, there are several reasons families may decide not to proceed with an intervention, one common one is the lack of understanding of mind control and psychological manipulation. Hopefully, the meeting will rectify this problem.

THE OPTIONS

It is now time to consider the family's options. The issues involved include the primary decision to go ahead or not, the choice of exit counsellors and a range of practical issues, including timing, venue and cost.

The primary decision to go ahead or not is discussed in a later chapter. So too are the options in the event the family decides not to go ahead. If the family chooses to proceed, the choice of exit counsellors is crucial. The family would know best what type of person has the best chance of interacting with the cult victim. The gender, the personality and the general presentation of the exit counsellor will all affect the intervention. If there has been limited contact with the cult member since the person joining, the family will have to base their decision on the 'pre-cult personality', which may have changed quite substantially.

There are significant advantages in using more than one exit counsellor. However, this will affect the cost of the intervention. It is extremely helpful if the team can include an ex-member of the cult, who is best equipped to deal with the feelings of the cult victim. All too often the member will say, 'If only you had experienced what I did, you wouldn't be sitting here today.' It comes as a useful surprise when the exit counsellor can respond, 'Well, if you really want to know, I was in the same group for nine years before my family helped me, as your family is trying to help you today.'

I encourage the family to do their own research into the choice of exit counsellors. This can be done by contacting anti-cult agencies for references. You may be able to access the name of a person or family the exit counsellor has previously worked with, in order to gain some feedback about their methods, presentation and professionalism. Although some families will not discuss their situation with others, there are many who are only too happy to assist.

In any industry there will always be the charlatan or the fake. Within the cult arena, these people often surface after a big story has hit the headlines; families panic and rush into an ill-prepared plan of action. Remember that you won't call an exit counsellor today to find him on your front doorstep tomorrow. It can take weeks, possibly months, to organise all this. The wait can be frustrating, but it is certainly worthwhile waiting for an appropriate person rather than using somebody who is unknown and yet to be proven.

Practical issues

Timing must include any other events in the family's calendar. An intervention involves stressful and difficult times; there is little point in going ahead if grandmother is about to go into hospital or if a sibling is sitting her final examinations. It may also be useful to focus on the cult's timetable in order to choose a quiet period, when it will be easier for the person to be away from the cult. It will be very difficult to encourage the person to leave if the group is celebrating the guru's birthday or if a new group of recruits is being initiated. Conversely, it may be advantageous to organise the intervention around a family occasion, a birthday or anniversary. It may add an incentive for the person to be with their family.

The choice of *venue* is important. The farther it is from the cult centre, the better. I find that seaside or bush settings are particularly attractive, as they provide a space in which the cult victim can breathe freely, well away from the regimentation and regulation of the group. That feeling of freedom and space has been a major catalyst in assisting people I have exit counselled successfully.

Cost and *fees* must be discussed. Apart from the professional fees charged by the exit counsellors, there are travelling and accommodation expenses. There are incidentals such as food and drinks or the hire of a video machine. The cost of the intervention will also depend on whether the counsellors are local or from overseas. It is important for families to understand that interventions can cost thousands of dollars and to familiarise themselves with the various cost components.

GOAL CLARIFICATION

It is essential for the family to fully understand the scope of an intervention and to have a clear idea of what exit counsellors will do and will not do. The following summary is the key to a viable intervention plan. Without proper and comprehensive clarification of these goals, an intervention is likely to be doomed.

Exit counsellors will:

- offer the opportunity for a series of meetings with the cult member;
- present reliable and objective information about the particular group;
- provide a forum for discussion and debate about involvement in the group.

Exit counsellors will not:

- become involved in an involuntary intervention;
- attempt to *unduly* influence the cult member's decision to remain in the group or leave (for a discussion on the role of the exit counsellor in influencing the cult member's mind, see 'The Role of the Exit Counsellor in Reversing Mind Control')[2];
- offer a theological or spiritual alternative to the cult experience;
- act as a mouthpiece for the family.

GUARANTEES AND SUCCESS

I am amazed at how many people are prepared to go ahead with an intervention and find the funds to cover it as long as they know that it will be 'successful'. It is a common thread running through many of the calls received at Cult Counselling Australia. In part, this attitude may be a product of the media, which reports glamour stories of people who have left a cult and lived to tell the tale. Perhaps there is a tendency to apply the same black-and-white formula to the concept of intervention as the cults apply to life in general.

A brief word about success. Success can be defined as an effective intervention, whereby the former cult member relinquishes all ties with the cult. Unfortunately, if this is the definition of success, there can be no guarantees, even though most exit counsellors will not take on a case unless there are reasonable chances of the person leaving the group. These chances are usually in the range of 70 per cent.

However, if we define success more broadly, the rate jumps to close to 100 per cent. A broader definition of success must include improved communication with the cult member as well as a better understanding on their part that the family does care and does love them. Although they may not have shown any response to the family's efforts, many a former member has acknowledged the influence of these efforts even while still in the movement. Furthermore, because the preparation and actual intervention are a family affair, invariably, regardless of the outcome in terms of the cult member's ability to be extricated from the group, the family gains enormously from the experience, on both an individual and collective level. The awareness and the insights gained can create permanent change and, if anything, pave the way for an improved relationship with the cult member — which may improve the chances of them leaving the cult of their own volition, or open the way to another intervention attempt.

Finally, a word of advice. Before commencing this long journey, the family must be emotionally prepared for what lies ahead. It is going to be a difficult time, bringing new experiences and new challenges. An intervention calls for an enormous input of energy; it is an emotional challenge. If the family is not strong and united, it is going to be difficult to develop a comprehensive strategy, get organised and follow through with the plan.

I usually give families between a week and a month to think about all the implications of the meeting and suggest they get together on their own as a family to make a decision. Unlike the cult victim about whom they are concerned, they need to be able to make an informed decision, which may be one of the most difficult of their lives, but which may bring about the most singularly significant change any family member can ever experience.

PART 6

THE INTERVENTION — Coming Home

- DEBBIE AND THE MYSTIC FROM POONA

- MICHAEL AND THE ASSEMBLY OF LIGHT

  AND TRUTH — A MOTHER TELLS

- EXIT COUNSELLING — REVERSING MIND CONTROL

For many families, the idea of an intervention can be quite overwhelming. Parents express fear about a process that may create significant change over a short period of time. Some compare the fear with the lack of certainty and the worry felt if a child requires surgery. 'Will the operation be successful? Will it work? Have we made the right decision?'

It is common for parents to agree to an intervention on the condition 'that it will work'. They question our 'success rate', which is a fair enough question, but every situation is different. It may be necessary for several meetings with the cult victim before any progress can be made. In other situations, everything may take place at the one meeting.

I find it particularly difficult to convince parents that there are no guarantees of success and that the intervention process is extremely valuable even if the results are below their expectations. Because the costs of interventions can be relatively high, it is understandable for families to expect results. What is achieved does not always match up to these expectations.

In the following chapters I document two interventions in which I played a part. In both cases, the interventions were successful; nevertheless, the nature of the cults and the circumstances of the interventions were very different.

Debbie's situation includes her own testimony about how she felt during the intervention. In Michael's case, his mother describes her feelings, doubts and misgivings about a very difficult process.

Debbie's story was particularly interesting because of the media coverage it received. Quite apart from a rather angry response from the Rajneesh group, the publicity appeared to encourage many other cult victims to seek help, knowing that they were not alone.

Following Debbie's and Michael's stories, I attempt to show how exit counselling actually works, the various methods that are used and the means by which the results are achieved.

In writing this section and documenting Debbie's and Michael's stories, I hope to remove some of the mystery surrounding exit counselling and to reassure families of the human and dignified nature of this delicate process. This understanding is vital in helping families decide whether to go ahead or not.

CHAPTER 23

DEBBIE AND THE MYSTIC FROM POONA

The story of Debbie's escape from Rajneesh is a true account of her experience in the group as well as the intervention that saw her released from it. Names have been changed for anonymity.

DEBBIE JOINS THE ORANGE PEOPLE

Debbie had joined the Rajneesh group, known also as the Orange People, whilst travelling in Byron Bay in northern NSW. Although initially her husband, Raymond, considered Debbie's involvement with an alternative group as an opportunity to experience a different lifestyle, he became increasingly concerned as Debbie's correspondence became vague and confusing.

Debbie also spoke about the possibility of travelling to India to spend time in a Rajneesh ashram. At this stage, her husband was uneasy about how 'happy Debbie had become', because it didn't sound genuine. It was as if Debbie were repeating catch phrases and clichés that the group had imposed on her.

When Raymond or her parents tried to speak to her logically or be rational with her, they were accused of being on a 'head trip'. There were strong undertones of 'this is the way, the only way' and a lack of tolerance for anyone else. Her friends felt that Debbie was becoming isolated from them.

As her husband became more concerned about Debbie's situation, he was directed to an organisation called The Jewish Centre, which was operating in Melbourne. I had helped establish the organisation in the late 1970s to respond to a growing concern about the spread of religious cults. The Centre also provided services in the field of exit counselling.

I conducted several meetings with Raymond and Debbie's family in order to gain information about the family background and an understanding of Debbie's situation. It was also important to educate the family on the issue of cultism, with particular reference to the Rajneesh group. We discussed the idea of exit counselling as well as the possibility of developing a strategy that could be implemented to assist Debbie. This discussion included practical issues, such as a venue for exit counselling, timing and costs.

It was clear that Debbie would not respond to Raymond's invitation to participate in a counselling session. It was therefore necessary to find a facilitator who could encourage her to do so. Because she had cut herself off from many of her friends, our choices for a facilitator were limited. We were, however, successful in convincing a long-time friend, Jenny, to assist.

Jenny knew very little about cults, but was willing to learn. She read the few letters that Debbie had written to her family and was convinced that 'this was not the Debbie she knew'. She hoped that her earlier friendship would still allow her to establish the rapport needed to assist her. This was going to be particularly difficult, because Debbie was living in the Perth ashram, and the intervention was to take place in Melbourne.

The exit counsellor to be used in the intervention was Robert, a former member of Rajneesh. Jenny was introduced to Robert and the strategy was discussed in detail. Robert would take responsibility for the counselling once Debbie had arrived. However, he felt it would be highly advantageous if Jenny could stay. She could act as both a support for Debbie and, if necessary, a back-up for Robert. Jenny would also try to gain some feedback from Debbie as to how she felt about Robert and the counselling.

The plan was for Jenny to travel to Perth to meet with Debbie and convince her to return to a farmhouse in Victoria to spend time together. Jenny was aware of the possible difficulties in convincing Debbie to leave the ashram. A number of options were discussed. It was also agreed that if Debbie were adamant that she could not leave, Jenny would try to talk to her in Perth, in order to strengthen their bond as the basis for a future attempt at an intervention.

After one further meeting with Debbie's husband and parents, Jenny travelled to Perth. At the ashram she asked to see Debbie. It wasn't until she mentioned Debbie's new spiritual name that anybody bothered to look for her. When Debbie did finally arrive, she seemed very distant. It was hardly the sort of meeting one would expect for two people who had been the closest friends throughout school and were now seeing each other for the first time in five years!

Although Debbie was suspicious about Jenny's motive for seeing her, Jenny directed the discussion to her own problems, in particular, the fact that she had just terminated a four-year relationship. Speaking of her own loneliness and isolation, Jenny was able to convince Debbie to return to Melbourne in order to spend some time together. 'I couldn't believe it when she said yes,' Jenny said later on. 'I wasn't sure whether she saw me as a potential convert to Rajneesh, or whether she recognised that she too had problems.'

Debbie was afraid to leave the ashram without permission. Perth was a very long way from Melbourne. Jenny said that she would take responsibility and suggested they leave at lunchtime when less people were around. In an attempt to reassure Debbie that she would return, Jenny told her to leave all her belongings at the ashram. Later that day, they caught a taxi to the airport and flew to Melbourne.

'It was only during the flight that I realised how Debbie had changed. The changes went far beyond the orange clothes she was wearing and the mala she wore around her neck. Debbie was no longer Debbie. She had a spiritual name, a new birthday and, most importantly, a new family. Despite the claim that "she was happy" and saw no need for the support of her family and friends, she seemed very alone. Her marriage could hardly be described as a relationship; she had grown very distant from Raymond. On one hand, she appeared extremely vulnerable; on the other, she seemed to be devoid of feelings and emotion.

'Her veneration for the guru, Bhagwan, was unbelievable. He was everything, a leader, a father and the "person" she now loved most. She appreciated the fact that Bhagwan had told the sannyasins (followers) not to think; she was intrigued by his statement that "sex was the first rung on the ladder to enlightenment". I tried to delve deeper but got nowhere.

'From time to time, Debbie would completely tune out and I had to wait until she had finished a meditation until we could talk again. Some of the changes in her were very subtle, others were more obvious.

On landing in Melbourne, Jenny told Debbie that she was now living on a farm in central Victoria and that they could spend some time in this very peaceful setting. Debbie agreed, but reminded Jenny that she had to be back in Perth the following day at the latest. 'I don't want to be reported missing; as it is, I'm so scared.'

Later that evening Debbie and Jenny arrived at the farm. Jenny had intended telling Debbie about the exit counselling, but Debbie was too tired. She decided to leave it to the next day. Her first task had been to get Debbie back to Melbourne. That had been accomplished. The next day would be the big test.

Day One: Debbie Meets the Exit Counsellor

Debbie's first activity the next day was a meditation. Later on, she revealed that she had prayed to Bhagwan to protect her and to ensure that if this were a test, she would survive. She had prayed that Jenny would 'see the light' and come back to Perth to dedicate her life to Bhagwan.

Debbie appeared very peaceful. She knew that it was only a matter of hours until she would be back at the ashram.

At breakfast, Jenny talked to Debbie about their friendship and how it was wonderful to be together again, especially after their lives had taken such different directions. She recalled their schooldays and the holidays their families had enjoyed together. She had brought her old photos and showed them to Debbie. There were pictures from their rock-climbing expeditions, the swimming competition and the school graduation ceremony.

At times, Debbie seemed to lighten up, but generally she was somewhat passive and introspective, with very little to say.

Jenny wasted no time in telling Debbie that her family was concerned and that although her instinct was to discount their concern, she too had questions about Debbie's newfound path in life. She talked about the distance she felt with Debbie and the fact that their meeting the day earlier had been so emotionless.

Debbie was unmoved, telling Jenny that she was fine and happy and that if Jenny would take the plunge, she could come back with her. Debbie had a new vision of life and a new reality that no longer required the family relationships which were once important. 'It's just a matter of time, you'll see, the world will see.'

Jenny asked Debbie why she had been so afraid to come to Melbourne with her and why she needed to return to Perth so soon. She asked her whether she was still as close with her parents and, in particular, with her sister. Referring to Bhagwan, she asked Debbie when she had seen him last and what she had learnt from the experience.

Debbie's answers to all the questions were very vague and noncommittal. At times, she would close her eyes and meditate as if she had to connect to another source in order to find the answers. Throughout the discussion she was holding her mala. She had placed a picture of Bhagwan on the table and kept glancing at it from time to time. After Jenny had finished speaking, Debbie said, 'Is that it, can we go now?'

Jenny responded, 'No, Debbie, we aren't going now. We are here to work this out. We are here to talk and as soon as we talk, we can go back. But I have invited someone else to this meeting. His name is Robert and he used to belong to the same group you belong to. He also wore the orange clothes and the mala. He travelled to India and lived in the ashram for two years. And now I want him to talk to both of us.'

Debbie said she needed to meditate again and walked outside. Some 30 minutes later she returned, looking far more confident and reassured. 'Bhagwan has said that we can talk, but only briefly, because he is calling me back.' Jenny suggested that they lunch together and they could talk after that. Debbie said she wasn't hungry but agreed to sit with Jenny while she ate.

'For some inexplicable reason, lunch gave me the first real opportunity to look at Debbie. Although we had spoken in Perth and travelled together, I hadn't really looked at her face, her eyes. Now I knew something was wrong, although I had no way of communicating this to Debbie. The feeling and emotion, the life and the energy simply weren't there. I was thankful that if we were successful, there was a chance Debbie would leave the ashram for good.'

Robert introduced himself to Debbie over lunch. He said that he had been involved in Rajneesh for many years, had spent time in India and travelled extensively. 'Since then, I have made it my goal to talk to other sannyasins about Rajneesh, and I really want to talk to you.' Robert was looking Debbie in the eye. She smiled back. Something seemed to register with her and she started laughing. It wasn't a natural laugh.

'Are you here to talk me out of Rajneesh? Well, do you want to start now? I'm about to go back to Perth, so you'd better be quick. Maybe you want to come back with me.' Debbie started laughing again.

Robert listened and continued, 'No, Debbie, I'm not here to talk you out of anything. I'm here to tell you about my own experiences and to share information with you. What you do with my experiences and that information is your decision.' Debbie seemed relieved. Robert was very pleasant. He continued, 'I'm a counsellor. Your family is concerned about you. Jenny is also really upset. They want to sort things out and they've asked me to help them.' Robert again reiterated that it was up to Debbie to decide what she wanted to do.

'If I tell you my story, you will understand better. I know your ashram well. I also lived in Fremantle for over a year. It's a beautiful place; it's filled with beautiful people. I learnt to love Bhagwan; I gave him everything. I had become disenchanted with Christianity and I was looking for direction. Bhagwan gave me so much that I gave him everything I had, including a house and small shop which I had inherited from my grandparents.

'I had never seen Bhagwan; it wasn't until I arrived in India when I received sannyas that I saw Bhagwan. Even though I believed in him from the first day I arrived at the ashram in Perth, seeing him was just something else.' Robert spoke warmly about his travels and experiences in India.

For a moment Debbie seemed confused; it was as if on one hand she had an ally with whom she could identify, and on the other, a counsellor who wanted to 'share information'. She seemed to find comfort in the fact that Robert had actually seen Bhagwan, as if that gave him a stamp of approval. She was listening, but kept slipping in and out of her meditation and appeared tired. Robert asked her if she would like to have a rest. Debbie was quick to agree and slept for two hours.

Dinner was served late and it was not until 8 p.m. that everybody sat down again to talk. Debbie seemed more alert and quite willing to sit down with Jenny and Robert. Robert saw that she had been listening to his story; he decided he would continue. He knew it was important for her to know that he had left the Orange People.

He explained how initially as a university student he had become attracted to the Rajneesh movement. He was studying Fine Arts at the time. 'It didn't take long until I had moved into an ashram. I actually broke off all contact with my family. Not everybody does that, but I felt it was the only way I could really be with Bhagwan. What attracted me to Rajneesh was the lack of structure. It was like a "non-religion". Everything was done for the moment. It was totally experiential. That's what counted.

'Eventually, I travelled to Poona and lived there for two years. Everything was fine, I thought I was happy. Then I received the news my father was dying, and my family wanted me to come home. I didn't go home. I didn't hear about his death until a month after he died. A week later, my old university lecturer was passing through India. He had a letter from my parents and a picture of my father.'

Robert continued, 'My lecturer asked me a whole lot of questions. He asked me about the funeral. He wanted to know if I had graduated. He asked me about my girlfriend. He asked me if there were anything I wanted to send to my mother. He would take it for me. He was interested in the Rajneesh philosophy and asked me all about it.

'I can't remember how I answered my lecturer. That part is still hazy, but I do remember the following night. I recall going through the questions one by one. The funeral? I hadn't even bothered to attend. My parents were no longer significant. My graduation? I had dropped out of university the day I walked into the ashram for the first time. My girlfriend? I had been with Deanne for four years, but I don't think I even said good-bye to her. What did I want to send to my mother? What mother? She was no longer part of my life.

'That night I started thinking. It was particularly difficult as I wasn't allowed to think. Thinking was called a "head trip", and you weren't meant to do it. I realised that from the time I had become involved in Rajneesh, my brain had shut down.

'I felt that God had sent my lecturer to wake me up. It was very scary, because I suddenly felt all alone. I wanted to ask the other sannyasins whether they felt the same as I did, but I knew that I would just get pulled under again. So I decided to leave the ashram and continue travelling. But within days I was struck by the enormity of the Rajneesh experience and how I had almost lost my mind. I couldn't continue travelling. I returned to Australia and went into therapy for six months.

'Since then, I have recommenced my studies, I'm involved in a relationship and I see my mother quite frequently. Life isn't as exciting as it was in Poona, but it's a real challenge.'

Debbie looked quite frightened. She couldn't look at Robert. She was holding her mala in her hand, not quite knowing what to do. Robert felt he had given Debbie plenty to think about. He asked her if she wanted to say anything; she said she didn't know.

It was time to go to sleep. Jenny offered to speak to Debbie, but she asked to be left alone. It had been a very long day.

DAY TWO: MIND CONTROL, BHAGWAN AND DEBBIE

Although Robert usually raises the issue of mind control at the end of the second day, in this instance he felt that it would be preferable to mention it earlier. He was concerned that Debbie might leave the next morning. By bringing up the issue of mind control he hoped to accomplish two things. Firstly, he felt that the issues might draw her into the discussion. Secondly, in the event of her deciding to leave, she would have at least picked up this important information.

Robert's concern arose out of Debbie's silence and her unwillingness to be an active participant in the discussions. He wondered whether she was so shut off that he wasn't reaching her. On the other hand, he felt that the previous evening had been worth while. He had wanted to get through his story and explain to Debbie why he had left the Orange People. He felt reasonably sure that she had got the message.

After breakfast Jenny asked Debbie about Bhagwan. Debbie responded straight away. 'He is the most beautiful being I have ever met. I am in love with him. I have never experienced anything like it.' Jenny asked her when she had last seen Bhagwan and what they had spoken about. Debbie answered that she didn't need to see Bhagwan in order to be with him. She then slipped back into a meditative trance.

Robert turned the talk to the meditation techniques used at the ashram. 'Do you remember the meditations? Do you remember the gourishankar meditation? I do. We had to look at a flashing strobe light for so long that I lost it. There were the floatation tanks where we would stay for hours at a time. I felt sick after those meditations, really sick.

'Why are you so scared? Happy people aren't scared. You are scared of going back to Perth late, because the people who love you so much and love everybody else won't let you spend time with your friend, who really loves you. I remember being scared when I was in Orange. It used to bother me, but I wasn't allowed to think about it.'

Debbie was beginning to feel agitated and uncomfortable. She turned to Jenny and suggested that they go outside. Later on she described how she began to panic. She realised that Robert was asking the right questions, which she couldn't answer. Meditating didn't seem to act as adequate protection. She felt vulnerable and exposed. She even thought of running away.

Robert came outside and asked Debbie if she was all right. Debbie said she was fine but told him she needed to get back to Perth. Robert said that it wouldn't be long until she could decide whether she wanted to return to Perth.

He knew that at last he was reaching Debbie and that she was listening to him. The smile and the veneered composure were gone. In their place a picture of an anxious and vulnerable young woman was emerging. Robert realised that if Debbie were going to leave, now would be the time. He continued the discussion. He asked her what she knew about Bhagwan and his background. He questioned whether the naturopathic drops she was taking might contain drugs. He asked her how it was possible that so many high-ranking Rajneeshies had been charged with corruption. He wanted to know how it was possible for a spiritual guru to live in such wealth whilst his disciples slept on the floor in the ashrams.

'Do you know about the 20-year contraception plan? Do you know that hundreds of women have been sterilised as part of Rajneesh's plan to prevent overpopulation of the world?

Debbie, do you want to be sterilised? Bhagwan talks about love; can there be love in a childless world?'

Robert suggested they go for a walk to give Debbie a chance to tell her story. She told how her parents did not believe in religion and how she had always yearned for spirituality. She told Robert of the problems she was having in her marriage and how she had decided to travel in order to get away. 'Rajneesh was the answer, I felt he was a gift from God. It feels so good.'

Robert asked her about her family. She was very ambivalent about her parents. Her level of contact with them was decreasing She admitted that the relationship with Raymond was in trouble.

It was getting late and everyone was getting tired. Debbie asked Jenny if they could talk by themselves. For the first time she admitted she was confused and she didn't know what to do. She seemed to be looking to Jenny for help in making a decision. Jenny responded quickly. 'I won't make a decision for you, I told you in Perth that we were going to Melbourne to talk. I'm so glad we're here. But maybe the difference between all of this and your Rajneesh experience is that here *you* make the decisions.'

Just before they went to sleep, Debbie asked Jenny, 'Do my parents know I'm in Victoria?' This was the first time she had initiated any discussion about her parents.

Day Three: The Turning Point

The next morning Jenny and Robert saw that Debbie was very distressed. It looked as though she hadn't slept at all. Debbie told Jenny that she didn't know what to think any more. She would stay the day and go back the following day. This was the first time she had ignored the 'fear' of going back late.

'Now it's your turn, Debbie,' Robert said. 'You talk to me. Ask me some questions.' Debbie was taken aback and said she really had nothing to say. Robert prompted her again. Finally, she asked him how he had become involved in this whole story. She had forgotten that this had been explained at the beginning of the meeting. Robert explained again how her parents had been concerned about her, how they had contacted him to counsel Debbie.

'Debbie, when you became involved in Rajneesh, did they tell you that you would probably lose contact with your family and friends? Did they tell you about the meditations? Did they tell you would have to clean toilets and call that a meditation too? Did they tell you that you would have to hand over most of your dole money to the ashram? Did they tell you about the corruption in the organisation?'

Debbie was visibly upset and, for the first time, started crying. Robert left the room, leaving Jenny with Debbie. Debbie wouldn't stop crying and asked to be left alone. A few minutes later, Jenny came back into the room. 'Maybe I should call Raymond,' she said.

Jenny called Raymond and put him on the phone. But Debbie couldn't speak. She hung up the phone. 'I'm so confused, I don't know what to do.' Robert suggested that she take a break or have a rest.

Robert offered to show Debbie a video. Together they watched *Thy Will Be Done*. Debbie was struck by the similarities between her story and the testimonies in the documentary. She asked Robert, 'What happens next?' Robert asked her whether she would like to go home to Raymond or to her parents. Debbie felt that it would be difficult returning to her husband at this stage. She chose to go to her parents' home. She asked whether Robert would explain to her parents what had happened. He suggested that she do the explaining but that he would make himself available if they wanted to ask any further questions.

Debbie was still concerned that the Orange People would find her. Jenny said that she would contact them and explain that Debbie was not coming back. She also said that a friend of hers in Perth would organise the return of her clothes and other belongings. Robert asked Debbie whether she would like to go over the events of the past few days. He felt that although she was now out of the group, she didn't have a grasp of the concept of mind control. Debbie agreed and together they reviewed the intervention.

Every few minutes, Debbie came up with another question. She recalled the time when everyone in the group had been asked to fill out a social security form. Now she understood that the form allowed the automatic transfer of their financial benefits to Rajneesh. She remembered that during the early days in Orange, she had contacted her friends to tell them where she was. She had not received responses from any of them. Now she realised that their letters had not been forwarded to her.

Robert advised Debbie to find a counsellor who understood cultism and would be able to assist her in the coming months. He also suggested that, if possible, she join a support group.

It was clear to Robert that Rajneesh had helped fill the spiritual void in Debbie's life and that this issue would need to be addressed in the early days of the recovery process. She had not resolved a number of issues relating to her past; she would have to deal with her marriage situation. Debbie also knew that now it was not the time to address those issues. Robert said that he would find a time in the coming days to review Debbie's options for counselling.

Jenny agreed to stay with Debbie at her parents' home for the following week. Later that afternoon, Robert left the house and Jenny and Debbie travelled to her parents' home. She spoke to them for the first time in almost a year.

FREE FROM THE CULT, DEBBIE TELLS HER STORY

Following her release from the Rajneesh group, Debbie described her experiences in a lengthy media interview.

'I was staying in a place in New South Wales and I met a couple of young guys who were into Bhagwan. One of the guys started talking to me about the movement and we went for a walk one night and he really looked beautiful in his flowing orange robes. His calmness and quiet way of answering all my questions really attracted me. My marriage was in trouble and I guess I was a bit vulnerable.

'This guy had been with the Orange People for four years. I left him that night feeling very warm and peaceful. He seemed to have the answers to questions I had been asking for years. It didn't cross my mind that he might be involved in a cult because of the way he expressed things. He didn't push me into anything.

'He went away for a week and when he came back, he said he was travelling to Perth for a "celebration". I said I might come because I wanted to see what it was like. The day before we left, I said, "Okay, I'll take the jump and wear orange." I borrowed some of his wrap. The orange makes you feel as if you belong and outsiders look at you differently. I certainly felt different.'

In Perth, Debbie officially joined the Orange People and went to live in one of the small houses near the ashram. She was on the dole, which she gave to the ashram, saving $10 for herself. 'You give them all your possessions, but you are not forced to do it. You hand them over because you love the people and you love Bhagwan.

'For the first week I spent the days cleaning toilets and bathrooms. It was really hard work because everything had to be spotlessly clean. I got a bit depressed, but they kept telling me that this was all part of the process of renewal. At night we had to do one hour of special meditation and then after dinner we'd watch videotapes of Bhagwan. In bed at night I'd sometimes go to sleep listening to tapes of him speaking.

'The following week I had a very bad experience with a meditation which involved staring at a flashing blue strobe light for fifteen minutes. At the end of it, I didn't know where I was. The next day I was too sick to get out of bed, and even now I get upset when someone takes a photograph of me with a flash. By the middle of the week, I felt like a new person.'

Although Debbie made it clear that she wasn't into sleeping around, she did tell of two girls who were forced to have sex, a claim later on denied by the Rajneesh movement. 'The sex thing is a big part of the scene because Bhagwan believes that sex is a way of achieving oneness, of losing your ego.

'Most of the people there are very loving, very beautiful people, but they have been duped. They have lost their minds, just like I have lost mine. That's why now I hate Bhagwan. He is robbing innocent people of their lives and their truth and feeding them lies. He is an amazing man. He has lots of charisma and he is very gifted. He knows a lot of psychology. I was really convinced that he was God, and I thought he was creating new people. Now I know that God doesn't want you to lose your mind. He gave me a mind so that I could think for myself. That's what I'm doing now.'

Debbie says that during the exit counselling she was never held against her will, but admits that she thought of flying back to Perth as soon as she discovered the real reason Jenny had invited her to Melbourne.

'I laughed at them when they told me what was going on. I told them how happy I was, how beautiful the Orange People were, and how Bhagwan and his followers were going to change the world. I really believed that. But they knew everything about the Orange People and they went through it, point by point.

'Then slowly the things I was being told started sinking into my brain, and I started thinking for myself again. I started wondering about the money side of the movement. I started asking myself whether Bhagwan really was God. I kept wanting to see some of my friends from the ashram, people who I thought could answer some of the criticisms that were being made of the Orange organisation.

'But then I thought, "Why can't I think for myself? Why can't I respond to the criticisms?" It was then that I realised I had been programmed to stop myself from thinking. My true feelings started coming out and I started to feel good and very, very relieved. My head started to clear. It was as if my brain had been turned around in the wrong direction and now it was being turned back again.

'Now I would like to do what I can to get other young people out of cults. I know I've been lucky … lucky that my parents cared enough and lucky they knew whom to go to for help. I'm now working at my job, and my life is coming back together again.'

Although Debbie had left Rajneesh, she also knew that the process of recovery would take time. 'The fact that my counsellors would remain in contact and be available after hours was very comforting; I don't think I would have made it without them.'

Debbie felt that there were many people to whom she owed her life. 'Without my parents' devotion, the rescue would not have been possible. Robert was fantastic.' But in another sense, Debbie's greatest appreciation went to Jenny. Debbie felt that Jenny's selflessness and courage were a major part of the whole experience.

'I remember looking at her during the early hours of the exit counselling, hoping that despite her concern about me, she would protect me. I think it would be fair to say that without her support I would have run away. Instead, I sat through it, although those few days were amongst the most difficult I have ever experienced. Once I could start crying again, I cried so much. Robert and Jenny were very gentle, but the information they were giving me was ripping me to shreds. In that respect, it was a very rough ride.

'I still have moments when I miss the people from the ashram. I still really love them and want to help them see the truth. I am scared that, somehow, I might be taken back. After getting out, there is this void, this emptiness, because you have had a false sense of fulfilment. You need help, and above all, you need lots of love. It's like kicking a drug habit.'

CHAPTER 24

MICHAEL AND THE ASSEMBLY OF LIGHT AND TRUTH — A MOTHER TELLS

The story of Michael and The Assembly of Light and Truth is a true account of a family's experience with a religious cult in Australia. However, for a number of personal reasons, the names of the family members, the exit counsellors and the cult have been altered.

'MUM, I WON'T BE COMING HOME' — THE BEGINNING OF A NIGHTMARE

Mum,

This letter will be short because there is not much time. Take it on board, lest you face the consequences.

It has become obvious to us all that The Assembly of Light and Truth will prevail. We are preparing for the revelation and are privileged to be part of it. There are only a few days left for you to join. If you choose not to join, you will be banished from the light and the truth. You will suffer as I did before I joined. I won't be coming home again until I am fully cleansed and strong enough to face the forces of evil. Heed my word today. There may not be a tomorrow for you.

In prayer and supplication,

Michael

The letter arrived on 5 May 1994. It was the first communication we had received from Michael since he had left home on Australia Day the previous year.

Later on that evening at dinner I read the letter to my husband, David, and my other two children, Ian and Melonie. Melonie, who was 17 at the time, said the letter must be a prank. Michael had a great sense of humour and he'd probably turn up the next day laughing. Ian wasn't so sure; neither was I. David had already rung the local Citizen's Advice Bureau in order to find out about cult counselling groups, but there were no listings. He had also contacted our local doctor as well as our Member of Parliament. Our joint efforts did not seem to be getting us anywhere.

The letter left us with so many questions. 'How had Michael suffered in the past? Had he been brainwashed about his childhood? What did he mean by being "banished"? By "only a few days left"?' This wasn't the Michael we knew.

We tried to remember the last weeks of Michael's life at home. Everything had been normal. He had been enrolled at university and working part-time. He was getting on well with us and his friends and was about to go camping for the summer holidays. We hadn't heard from him in the early part of January and figured that he was out of range, enjoying the mountains and the outback.

I had heard about cults. Both overseas and in Australia, there had been reports of cult activity, including death and suicide. I recalled seeing some of the groups fundraising, but I had difficulty in superimposing Michael's face on this image. It was as if he had just vanished and there was no one there to help us. And anyway, the cult theory was a longshot. Michael had no interest in religion and had hardly ever been to church.

My local bookshop was very useful. I was directed to Steve Hassan's book, *Combating Mind Control.* The book included the names of the few Australian agencies involved in cult work. At the time, the term 'exit counselling' meant nothing to me. For me, cults conjured up images of Jonestown, the Hare Krishnas at overseas airports, exotic clothes and powerful, wealthy gurus. That was the extent of my knowledge.

The research into Michael's whereabouts was painstaking, but it did not take long until we tracked him down at a church called The Assembly of Light and Truth. Situated in the Adelaide hills, the church had a membership of some 20 followers and was led by a man who was called The Pastor. If he had a name, very few people knew it. The so-called philosophy of the movement was a mixture of Christian theology with an eastern mystical slant and an emphasis on the end-times.

We were directed to an anti-cult agency operating in Melbourne. Known at the time as Free Minds, the agency was involved in counselling families in relation to cult matters. They also assisted in co-ordinating interventions.

I recall my relief after the first meeting. I was relieved that there were people who could assist. I had flown alone to Melbourne for the first meeting, as David and the kids were not yet needed. But we did meet together as a family during the following week.

The legwork was very time-consuming. Lengthy forms had to be filled out, followed by an exhausting orientation meeting. We spent hours looking at various options and strategies. We were put in contact with several exit counsellors in America.

The time difference between America and Australia meant that we had to stay up at all hours just to talk to the counsellors.

We read at least half a dozen books, we watched several videos. I felt I was becoming an expert in cultism in a matter of several weeks. We were told how to relate to Michael in the event that he attempted to communicate with us. The issue turned out to be academic, as Michael didn't contact us. Instead, just prior to the exit counsellors leaving the USA, Melonie approached Michael at the church and begged him to participate in a family meeting. Miraculously, he agreed on the condition he could go back to the church the following day.

I have never been able to understand why Michael did in fact agree to participate in the meeting. For me it was God showing His face. For others it may have been Michael's recognition that the church was not all light or truth, as the name suggested.

Exactly ten weeks after we had received Michael's letter, two exit counsellors arrived in Australia to conduct the intervention.

DAY ONE: BREAKING THE ICE

The first step in the intervention was our team meeting. By the team I refer to David and myself, my daughter, Melonie, my son Ian, as well as the two exit counsellors, Kevin and Shelley. We met at a friend's home where there was no possibility of a chance meeting with our son Michael.

The meeting lasted four hours. It was draining. Although we had communicated with the exit counsellors by phone and fax, this was the first time we had met and sat down together. The reality of the intervention was quite daunting.

Kevin was pleased that Michael was prepared to attend the intervention. Kevin said he would tell Michael that he and Shelley were exit counsellors and the meeting was an opportunity to exchange information. Kevin would assure Michael that he could leave at any time and that he and Shelley would not put any pressure on him.

We discussed accommodation. Although Kevin and Shelley had been staying at a motel, they suggested that they move over to the country house where the intervention was to take place. They felt that this would allow them to have more casual contact with Michael, especially if he were having doubts.

Kevin asked us whether we had any questions. Although I had been through this before, I felt I had to ask, 'But what if he runs out or it doesn't work?' Shelley acknowledged the possibility of this happening and reiterated that this was the risk we had to take. However, the country house was relatively isolated and we were meeting in the evening. Even if Michael wanted to leave, it would be difficult. There was no phone at the house, so he would have difficulty contacting The Assembly.

Later that afternoon our whole team travelled to the country house. It was arranged that Melonie would collect Michael from the nearest train station. Michael arrived on the scheduled train and was met by Melonie. He appeared drawn and nervous. He asked Melonie to reassure him that he would be going back to The Assembly the next day.

Melonie told Michael how well he looked and how the whole family was happy to be getting together. She told him that the counsellors were very understanding people and that she was sure he would relate well to them.

I recall my feelings when Michael walked inside. It was one of the moments during the intervention I will never forget. He looked around the room like a person facing daylight after having been in the dark for a long time. Despite all the preparation, nobody really knew what to do. I was afraid that he would sense my nervousness and the tension in the air. Melonie asked him if he wanted to eat dinner. He didn't hesitate.

We sat down to eat together with Kevin and Shelley. They both introduced themselves as counsellors and expressed their appreciation to Michael for being happy to participate in the meeting. The discussion turned to football and rugby. Michael still seemed very nervous; he certainly was very hungry.

Shelley explained how she enjoyed working with families and how she had come from a very abusive background. She referred to the fact that her parents were very controlling and gave her little space of her own. She said that eventually she had decided to take control of her own life and left home. 'That was the hardest decision in my life.'

Michael sat upright, his eyes fixated and staring ahead. 'May The Assembly of Truth and Light spread its countenance upon you. May we all surrender to the ultimate truth and light. May the countenance of truth and light fill the world. Amen.' After saying that, Michael relaxed again.

I looked at David. He understood my pain. This was our Michael who was now about to be initiated into The Assembly. Could we reach him? He looked so far away.

Kevin asked Michael about his life and what he had been doing over the past few years. Michael said he was a missionary and that he worked at various universities. He said that he had introduced many people to The Assembly. Kevin didn't ask any further questions, but said he'd be happy to hear more about Michael's life later on.

Later that evening everyone sat down together for the introductory meeting. Shelley opened the meeting by explaining that she and Kevin had been invited to talk about the family situation. She said that in her experience it was possible to work these sorts of things out; sometimes having an outsider there can help. Shelley asked me if I wanted to say anything.

I explained to Michael that we had had great difficulty in understanding Michael's religion. I told him that we had tried to do so by going to meetings and reading books about The Assembly. I explained how we could see that Michael's involvement with the church was affecting him and the whole family, and there were many things we couldn't understand. I pointed out that we rarely saw Michael alone and that on the few occasions we did, he was always rushing back to the church. I pointed out how his friends couldn't understand why he had dropped them so quickly. Why hadn't he attended his brother's 21st birthday and why was coming home for a family reunion so difficult?

I remember breaking down as I told him how much we loved him. It was eerie because he was staring right at me but didn't seem to respond. That was a very scary moment. 'Kevin and Shelley are counsellors who know about The Assembly and they know about our family,' I said. 'Now they want to help us get together like we used to be. Of course, you have grown up and we can't treat you like a child any more, but we can still be close and enjoy happy occasions together. The counsellors can give us information which we can discuss together as a family. This is a real opportunity.'

Michael stood up; he hadn't taken his eyes off me. 'The Assembly of Light and Truth is now meeting. We all see the light, we all know the truth. May we all be protected from the forces of evil. Amen.'

But then as quickly as he had stood up, he sat down and appeared to relax. 'I'm not sure about all of this. You want me to spend a few days with you. I'd like to take one day at a time. I hope that's OK with you.'

I was baffled. It was as if there were two Michaels at our meeting. For how long would this go on? I felt so overwhelmed. Michael seemed much worse than I had thought he would be. But, on the other hand, he had agreed to stay for at least another day. I tried to convince myself that everything would work out.

Later on, Melonie knocked on Michael's door and asked whether she could speak to him. Michael agreed, but as soon as Melonie came in, he turned the other way. He was praying, although this time he was speaking softly. After at least ten minutes he turned to Melonie. 'The Assembly of Light and Truth is now praying. Come pray with me. Pray for peace, pray for salvation, pray for harmony.' Melonie sat on Michael's bed and waited until he had finished. She looked at Michael; he half-looked at her. Melonie smiled, but Michael didn't respond. She felt lost and confused.

As she was about to walk out of the room, Michael called her back. 'I'm going back tomorrow, aren't I? I am leading the service over the weekend and I must be back.' Melonie didn't respond, but told Michael that she loved him so much and that she was glad the whole family was together.

DAY TWO: MICHAEL STARTS TALKING

After breakfast, David went for a walk with Michael. The rest of us regrouped for a quick meeting. Shelley said she was pleased with the progress, although Michael still seemed very connected with The Assembly. She said that the next meeting would be heavy, because she would talk about her own experiences in the church. Prior to doing so, they would watch the video *The Wave*. *The Wave* is an excellent production, which deals with mind control. We had all seen the video before.

Lunch was relatively relaxed and again Michael was very hungry. I thought to myself that if we couldn't get his mind in order, at least he'd walk out a healthier person. Then Michael popped the question to Kevin. 'Have you ever been involved in The Assembly?'

Shelley tried to be as nonchalant as possible. 'I was involved in The Assembly for four years, and I know a lot about them.' Michael was taken aback. For the first time he got angry, and my heart fainted. I wondered what would happen next and whether it was all over.

Michael ran to his room and took out his Bible and returned. Clutching it in his hand, he started another recital. 'And may those that have left The Assembly of Light and Truth repent or be banished for ever to the abyss of destruction. May Shelley repent and return. Amen.'

I remembered reading about the need to be prepared for the unexpected, and this unscheduled question was certainly an example. Shelley took over and asked whether we could give her a moment to speak to Michael.

'I can see you're upset,' she said. 'I was also upset when my parents introduced me to a counsellor who was a former member of The Assembly. I was angry, I wanted to run, I remember thinking that I will never forgive them. Look at me now, look at me today; am I any worse off for the experience? Why do you think we are here? Perhaps we have something to offer you. Has information ever been dangerous? Can I show you a video?'

Shelley said it appeared that Michael wanted to respond to her but didn't seem to know how. He seemed almost relieved to have the opportunity of seeing the video.

We all sat on bean bags and watched *The Wave*. I sat next to Michael. I didn't know what to do. Should I put my arm around him or not? The fact that I had to think about putting my arm around my own son made me feel sick.

Michael was unperturbed by my move. He was watching the video. I felt good because he didn't resist, but I was in pieces. Somehow, I was scared. We seemed to be getting so close. It was as if we were watching our son floundering in the ocean seas, trying to grasp onto something to keep him alive. But every time he found something, a big wave came and pulled him back. I just didn't know if we would make it, if *he* would make it. His recitals had sent a cold shiver down my spine.

The video had finished and Michael was still staring at the screen. I wasn't sure what was happening, but for Shelley this was just the moment she had been waiting for. She asked Michael whether he could just listen to her for a few moments. He agreed.

'I was a member of The Assembly. When I attended my first meeting, I wasn't told who they were. They were selling flowers for a charity which I now know didn't exist. They didn't tell me about the routine, the tithing and the prayer sessions. They told me they were my family and they restricted my contact with my parents and brothers and sisters. They married me off to a person I had never seen before. Our marriage lasted two years. Every day I had to raise funds well beyond my capacity. I remember almost collapsing on street corners whilst trying to fill my quota. I remember hating my parents. If I would have been told to kill them, I would have.'

I felt we were past the halfway point and prayed that nothing would go wrong. I could see that Michael didn't have the answers. Ian suggested that the family go for a walk. For the first time, we were a family again; the tension had gone and the walk was relaxed.

We didn't know what was on Michael's mind. What was he thinking? Could he see our point? Were we getting somewhere? Maybe he was just acting and was just pretending to comply with us. Kevin didn't think so. He felt that if Michael were trying to fool us, he would have been more responsive and would have already 'renounced his involvement'.

Clearly, Shelley's talk had made an impression on Michael. Together with *The Wave*, it seemed to have been a turning point. But I wondered where we would go from there.

That evening Michael said he wanted to talk to David and me. I asked him whether he would like to talk at the house or go for a walk. Michael said he'd rather stay at the house. We sat down on the verandah and asked him what he wanted to say.

'I don't understand what is going on,' Michael said. 'These counsellors you have brought here are very smart people and I can't help but think they are trying to brainwash me. It's very scary. They make a lot of sense and I really like Shelley; but I feel really strange. Maybe this is the first time in ages that I've asked you what to do, but that's what I'm doing right now.'

This was our Michael speaking again. There was a softness about the way he talked. Momentarily, at least, he seemed more gentle and less rigid. He was looking at us as he spoke.

My instinct was to reach out to Michael and to tell him to come home. I knew that was wrong, so I held back. I responded by telling him that he had to make the decision and that it might be worth while to talk to Shelley about her experience. I recall that moment as being very difficult. I felt bound by the counsellors' instructions not to manipulate Michael or influence him. But they were counsellors; they would never see him again anyway. We were his parents; couldn't we be honest with him, couldn't we bring him back? For the first time I was angry at Kevin and Shelley. I told David how I felt. He suggested I talk to the counsellors, which I didn't do.

I gave Michael a hug. It was the first time. I was crying, but he appeared unmoved. Was our optimism misplaced? Was he still so far away?

We were meant to meet again that evening, but we were all too tired. Kevin and Shelley suggested we wait until the next day. They felt we were making good progress. Somehow, I felt things were going too slowly. Maybe I was being selfish.

DAY THREE: MICHAEL AGREES TO LEAVE

The next morning Shelley and Michael went for a jog. Michael said it was great to be outside and breathe the fresh air. He seemed very happy and much more comfortable with himself. He told Shelley about his discussion with us the previous night and how I had suggested he talk to Shelley. He didn't mince his words. 'I'm so scared, I'm so confused. Should I leave or should I go back?' Shelley deliberately didn't respond and let him continue.

'You have given me so much information, but how can you tear me away from the church, from my friends, from my family? How can I just turn my back on them and leave? I have responsibilities I can't ignore.' Shelley remained silent for a moment and then asked, 'Michael, can you say that again, can you listen to what you are saying? Are you telling me that *we* are brainwashing you? Who's tearing you away?'

In the preparation for the intervention, I remember reading about the moment of 'snapping', the awakening of the real personality. Somehow, I had waited for that moment. I knew that when it came, it would make the whole process worth while. And, I missed it. It was at that moment when Shelley was with Michael that he woke up. Shelley explained how he had suddenly stopped in his tracks. He had looked at Shelley. It was as if now they had a common bond as ex-members of The Assembly of Light and Truth.

Once back at the house, Michael called David and me to his bedroom. He told them that it was over, he was leaving The Assembly. He seemed quite calm and again I wasn't sure how to react. I decided to trust my instincts and gave Michael a big hug. He responded. David asked what he wanted to do now. He said he didn't know. Clearly, he was not used to making decisions.

As soon as we came out of the bedroom, Kevin and Shelley spoke to Michael. To Michael's surprise, they spoke about the positive side of The Assembly and how he shouldn't forget the good times there and the lessons he had learnt. Shelley explained how she had felt, the confusion, the elation and the hope. She said they could speak about that later. Michael was exhausted and was relieved not to have to continue the discussion.

Michael said there was just one thing he wanted to do and that was to tell Melonie and Ian. Kevin, Shelley and I left the room and Michael called them over. He put his arms around Melonie and then Ian. They understood.

I peeped in through the curtain. I knew this was only the beginning, but that image of the three children together told me that we were going to make it. We did.

Michael did leave The Assembly. He underwent counselling for over a year. The family also participated in family therapy for several months. A year after the intervention, Michael travelled to the USA. At the time of writing, he has become involved in an anti-cult organisation in New York. Although he is not a primary exit counsellor, he does assist in interventions.

CHAPTER 25

EXIT COUNSELLING — REVERSING MIND CONTROL

Mind control involves a range of techniques which bring the cult member under the totalitarian rule of the group. The range of specialised methods and the way they are used by the cults have been discussed in earlier chapters.

Reversing the process requires an understanding of what contributed to mind control. There are many different techniques that have been developed since cultism attracted attention in its early days. There are no fixed rules and no two interventions are the same.

The process of reversing mind control involves numerous steps. In some respects the nature of the process will depend on the particular group involved. Although most groups use similar methods of recruitment and mind control, a closer assessment of the particular group will help finetune the relevant exit counselling approach.

This chapter attempts to demonstrate some of the techniques used by exit counsellors in reversing the process of mind control by referring to the experiences of Debbie and Michael described in previous chapters. The techniques include:

- The establishment of a rapport and trust between the exit counsellor, the team and the cult member.

- The involvement of the cult member as a partner in the exit counselling process.
- The opportunity for the cult member to re-identify with her/his pre-cult personality.
- The requirement that the cult member understand the concept of mind control.
- The ability of the exit counsellor to break down the 'all good/all evil' definition of the world.
- The ability of the exit counsellor to demonstrate the destructive nature of the group.

The first step in any intervention involves the establishment of *rapport and trust* between the cult member and the team. In the case of Debbie and the Orange People, well before Debbie had met the exit counsellors, Jenny had to convince her to travel from Perth to Melbourne with her. By talking about her own relationship problems, Jenny was indicating to Debbie that she trusted her. Jenny referred to her loneliness and isolation and spoke to Debbie as a confidante. When Robert, the exit counsellor met Debbie, he was quick to talk about his own experiences. At the same time, he was very honest about why he had been invited to the meeting and why it had been organised.

Neither Jenny nor Robert put any pressure on Debbie to say anything. It was only later in the evening — over twenty-four hours since Jenny had met Debbie and over eight hours since Robert had met her — that they started asking her questions.

In Michael's situation, Kevin and Shelley made sure the first meeting was at dinner-time. They talked about sport and about themselves. Shelley talked about her own past, in particular the fact that she had come from an abusive background. In doing so she had shown that everyone is vulnerable and there is no reason to feel embarrassed or guilty for events in your life over which you had no control.

Kevin was interested in hearing about Michael's life, but he didn't push the issue. Michael could talk later on if he wanted.

It is important that the person is able to feel *he or she is a partner in the process.* In the cult, the member had no control over events. The individual's life was regulated by the cult. Any breaks or rest time, for example, were part of the cult's agenda, into which the person had no input.

The first thing Debbie did when she woke up in the morning was to meditate. Jenny showed respect for her space and left her alone. Later in the afternoon, Robert asked Debbie if she would like a break and suggested that she decide when they could talk again. On the second day of the intervention, Robert asked Debbie to tell her story. Robert was saying that now it was her turn and the team really wanted to hear from her.

When, at the end of the first day, Michael said that he would like to take one day at a time, everybody agreed immediately. When Melonie wanted to speak to him in his room, she knocked first and asked Michael whether she could talk to him. The meeting planned at the end of the second day was cancelled because Michael was too tired to participate.

It is important that the team is able to get the cult member to *re-identify with the pre-cult personality.* Jenny went out of her way to talk about their earlier friendship and the things they used to do together. On several occasions she had Debbie recall memories of their times together, the naughty things they did, the time they ran away from school and the time they gatecrashed a party together. In Michael's story, Melonie chose the end of the second day to reminisce with Michael about their childhood and adolescence. She recalled the times they both ran away from the school camp only to have the police come after them, and the time when they were tricked into a blind date with each other.

Even though both Debbie and Michael slipped back into their cult personalities, the fact that they could, even momentarily, reconnect with their real personalities was a new experience and an important aspect of the intervention process.

It is important for the cult members to begin to understand the *concept of mind control*. Although this is an ongoing process, which will require further attention later on, it is also an integral part of the intervention. Robert was able to identify a number of practices and question Debbie about them. He used the examples of the 'head trip', the various forms of meditation and the fear in order to point out to Debbie that she was being controlled. He questioned Debbie's belief in Rajneesh as a perfect being when she hadn't met him and knew nothing about the manner in which he lived or the level of corruption in the movement.

Shelley's background with The Assembly was a powerful factor in the intervention. She was able to recount her experience of being controlled by the group. She was able to talk about her willingness to participate in fraudulent charity work, her marriage (which didn't last) and her absolute faith in the group and its mission. Her statement that she would have killed for The Assembly was also powerful. The use of *The Wave* further reinforced a model of mind control.

Debbie and Michael were able to internalise these questions and issues from a new position. Even though they were still very connected with their groups, they were physically away from them and able to look at them from a different perspective.

The team was able to *break down the 'all good/all evil' definition of the world*. For both Debbie and Michael, the people they met during the interventions were human beings. They did not appear satanic or instruments of the devil. As the intervention developed, Debbie was able to identify with Jenny as a friend and a confidante. She was able to listen to Robert and relate to him. Michael found his parents to be understanding and non-confrontational. He found a friend in Melonie for the first time in years. He also felt attracted to Shelley. His admission that The Assembly was a cult was made to Shelley, whom he had learnt to like and trust.

For both Debbie and Michael, the realisation that there are good people who do not belong to Orange People or The Assembly, was something very new. It threw into question one of the most basic principles of the cults' doctrines. It made them question their past behaviour and attitudes.

The corollary of this realisation was that 'there is life after the cult'. It was difficult for Michael to accept the fact that Shelley had belonged to The Assembly. If she had left as she said she had, she should have been killed in an accident or suffered serious injury. Her life should have been meaningless. Again the doctrine of the cult was seriously challenged.

Robert was able to demonstrate to Debbie how his life had come together after leaving the Orange People. His resumption of studies, his relationship with his mother and his involvement in a relationship were clear signs that it was possible to pick up the pieces and start again.

And finally, the team must show the cult members that the *group they belonged to was a destructive cult*. As the intervention proceeds, the team must connect the behaviour and practices of the group with the features of mind control which have been spelt out during the intervention. This realisation is a defining moment in the intervention process and usually precedes the moment of 'snapping', that is, the decision to part company with the group. In Michael's case it all came together when he was alone with Shelley. The experience of the past two days, a review of the cult practices and the definition of mind control, coupled with the fact that he was unable to identify Shelley as being evil, now gave Michael a clear message. He was able to renounce his affiliation with The Assembly.

It is important to note the different reactions of Debbie and Michael to the exit counselling process. Cults teach members how to avoid thinking. These techniques are used in the cult to block out negative thoughts. During interventions the same techniques are harnessed in order to avoid absorbing the theme of the intervention. Debbie tried to resist the intervention by meditating and focusing inwards. Michael resorted to the well-rehearsed recitals which he had memorised whilst in the group. In both cases, these practices became less as the intervention proceeded.

In concluding this chapter, a comment regarding 'snapping' is relevant. The literature on cultism discusses it as a definitive moment when the cult member relinquishes his ties to the group. The moment of 'snapping' is viewed as evidence that the reversal of the mind control is complete. The literature suggests that just as a person's indoctrination into a cult can be sudden, so too is the process by which the member departs from the group.

Although many cult members do snap out of the cult experience, others take more time. For these people, the intervention represents the beginning of a process which may take weeks or months. The cult member is committed to leaving the organisation; each day and each counselling session brings the person closer to the fulfilment of that goal. But the results are not immediate.

Whether the reversal of the mind control is more immediate or takes time, it is important to recognise that *all* former cult members are vulnerable and require support.

PART 7

WELCOME BACK TO THE REAL WORLD

- AFTER THE INTERVENTION — THE BEGINNING OF A

  NEW JOURNEY

- FEELINGS AND FEARS — LIVING WITH ONESELF

- INTEGRATION — RELATION TO THE COMMUNITY

- MARRIAGE, PERSONAL RELATIONSHIPS, DATING AND SEX

- WHAT ABOUT THE CHILDREN?

- AFTER THE CULT — THE FAMILY

There is something very exciting and special about meeting a former cult member after a successful intervention. In many years of working in different areas of counselling and therapy, I have found no parallel to match the experience of working in the cult scene.

Rosa and Trevor signed up for a personal development course. Although Rosa refused to participate in further training, Trevor did commit to several advanced courses. Their relationship appeared to be over. Trevor eventually suffered a breakdown. Rosa stood by him as he slowly recovered. They both travelled to a residential program in the USA. They have since returned to Australia. Each year, I am invited to their anniversary celebration, which marks the day they both returned to Australia and to each other.

After Joanna was finally removed from the clutches of Nora, we met at her home in Perth. Her family and I, together with Joanna, sat at the same table which had seen so many meetings without her presence. It was strange, almost eerie, to sit with her and to be near her, even more so for myself than her family.

I had not known Joanna before the intervention. To me, she was a series of photographs and the writer of numerous letters, which I had seen and studied. She was the subject of numerous meetings and hours of soul-searching. Like someone returning from the dead, now she was a person, smiling and alive.

I worked with Joanna for over a year. We had regular telephone appointments, initially twice a week, as well as meetings in Perth every three months. It took time until she was able to move beyond the highs and the lows, the depression and disorientation. It took time before she was able to enter into a relationship, move out of home and become independent.

Several years ago, I was involved in an intervention in New York in relation to an Australian girl, Sarah, who had become involved in The Family cult. Although the distance between Australia and the USA made the intervention difficult, I did attempt it. During the course of the intervention, Sarah excused herself and did not return. Neither her family nor I were aware of the fact that she had travelled back to Australia.

Several months later, I personally attended a meeting organised by The Family in order to track down a young man who had been recruited by the group. The woman at the desk who greeted me was Sarah. As surprised as she was to see me, she admitted her confusion regarding The Family and agreed to resume counselling where we had left off in New York. She left the group some weeks later and has not returned.

It is very easy for parents to assume that once out of the cult, the future will be positive. It is a dangerous assumption, which tends to ignore the difficult and is challenging times that lie ahead. This assumption also denies the family the opportunity to participate together with their loved one in the recovery process and ultimately to share the joy of personal independence and freedom.

CHAPTER 26

AFTER THE INTERVENTION —
THE BEGINNING OF
A NEW JOURNEY

'You are going to get frustrated and feel inept. Hear me again. You are going to get very frustrated and feel inept. You are going to feel as if you're walking on eggshells. Sometimes, the loved one will be sullen, sometimes he will explode for no apparent reason. Or, as my parents did, you will go into her room in the middle of the night to find her soaked with tears ... I can promise you, a healthy recovery will take longer than you expect.'[1]

The intervention and the exit counselling are only the first steps on a journey towards recovery and the regaining of independence. The journey can be painful and slow, requiring counselling, therapy and support.

Although various studies have been done, it is unclear as to the length of time it takes to recover from a destructive cult experience. It appears to depend on both the nature of the actual cult, as well as the length of time spent in its confines. In addition, it is necessary to assess the overall family situation and any unresolved issues which may have contributed to the cult involvement.

It is clear that there is an agenda of post-cult issues which must be addressed and that there are no shortcuts or means by which this process can be circumvented. I often receive calls from people who have left a cult many years earlier but who now seek counselling in relation to the effects of the experience. It can take years for former cult members to come to the realisation that this is necessary and that it is never too late to commence this work.

Some former members choose to participate in a residential program. These programs are designed to offer an intensive and structured method for dealing with the effects of the cult experience. They can be quite expensive. Other former members have re-integrated into society through the assistance of counselling and therapy, and make the transition from the totalitarian cult system to open society and democratic life.

Another option in addition to counselling is to join a group. In the same way that Alcoholics Anonymous and Narcotics Anonymous can serve as invaluable supports for former alcohol and drug addicts, so self-help groups too can provide substantial assistance for the former cult member.

Although some former members may choose to avoid counselling in the first few months after leaving the group, there are some situations which demand more immediate attention. In particular, where the member was exposed to any form of perverse sexual activity, rape, prostitution or serious abuse, it is advisable to seek advice from a psychotherapist and enter into therapy as early as possible. Because of the damage that such experiences can do to the former member, it is important for them to be dealt with earlier rather than later. In addition, the therapy will assist in the sphere of social interaction and integration as well as the formation of personal relationships.

In the event of the former members commencing counselling, it may be important for the counsellor to be available after hours and at other times, in case the client hits a low or feels vulnerable. Dr Margaret Singer makes the important distinction between the value of a trained exit counsellor and a general psychologist or psychiatrist:

'There are two reasons why exit counselling is preferable. Since exit counsellors understand how coercive persuasion works and how group influence and social pressure affect people's thinking, behaviour, spirit and emotions, they can educate the former member. They also understand and are able to explain some of the typical after-effects of meditation trance induction, intense coercion, pastlives regression, extensive blaming sessions, the destabilization of a person's sense of reality and other persuasion techniques used by the cults.

'Secondly, ordinary psychiatric and psychological counselling focuses almost exclusively on early life experiences and childhood history and the impact of these early years ... and gives almost no training that focuses therapists on adult experiences of intense social influences and group situations.'[2]

The choice of counsellor for ongoing work is so important that the options should be researched before making the first appointment. It may help to discuss this with the exit counsellor who was involved in the intervention. In the early days it may be possible for the exit counsellor to continue to work with the former member.

If another counsellor takes over, it is imperative that there be an appropriate 'handover' process. The former member has placed enormous trust in his exit counsellor. Unless the handover to the new counsellor is managed properly, the former member may feel a sense of rejection. Considering the erosion of his self-esteem by the cult, he may interpret the handover as a sign of his inadequacies or inferiority.

One of the most immediate issues requiring attention relates to the notion of 'floating'. Floating refers to the possibility of the former member returning to the state of consciousness which was apparent during the cult experience. Although the problem of floating may recede dramatically in the first few weeks, this is not always the case. It is an important feature of the post-cult experience and must be recognised.

The floating experience is usually triggered by certain sights, sounds, touches, smells or tastes in everyday life which remind the former member of an experience in the cult. 'Characteristically, floating occurs in cult members who have left the group of their own accord, have received incomplete counselling or are still in the beginning phases of counselling. A former member who floats after phoning a cult member may, as a result, even return to the cult.'[3]

In Debbie's case, one of the more powerful meditations in the Rajneesh group involved the use of a strobe light. After she left the group she found that she had to avoid all flash photography, because it created anxiety and stress.

Several years ago I was involved in assisting a young woman, Samantha, who had left a Christian fundamentalist cult. Although she had left of her own accord, she had never received counselling. Samantha had agreed to assist me in producing a video documentary of the testimony of former cult members. I had organised to pick her up in the morning and at the time I was driving a small white mini-bus. As Samantha stepped into the bus, she went pale and froze. She remained quite detached and non-communicative during the ride to the video site. She then managed to tell me that this bus resembled the vehicle her cult had used to distribute its members on street corners for fundraising. It took some time before she was able to regain her composure.

The best way to deal with floating is to discover the stimulus that creates the response. Obvious triggers include music that was sung or heard in the cult, prayers or chants, or a certain tone of voice. Triggers may be:

- Sights: special colours, flags, pictures of the leader, hand signals, facial expressions, symbols of the group, items used in group activities or rituals.
- Sounds: songs, jargon, slogans ... mantras ... speaking in tongues, curses, cue words and phrases.
- Touches: certain gestures or types of touching, handshakes, a kiss.
- Smells: incense, perfume or cologne of leader, food ...
- Tastes: certain foods, blood.[4]

Recognition of these triggers and the ability to respond to them requires learning and education. Certainly, the person who has managed to organise counselling will be far better equipped to identify these triggers and avoid any negative behaviour.

On a broader scale, the former member faces numerous challenges. For the purpose of this book I have divided them into two groups: the individual and personal challenges which affect the person in relation to her/himself, and those which are relevant to relations between the person and the community s/he lives in. These issues are dealt with in the next two chapters.

CHAPTER 27

FEELINGS AND FEARS — LIVING WITH ONESELF

'Even now, many years on, scenes from those days sometimes intrude in my dreams and I wake up at night in a fright, thinking I'm still at Uptop. Sometimes while working in the children's wards at the hospital, I hear a child screaming and my mind flashes back to Uptop and I get filled with irrational anxiety. I have to make an effort to calm myself and say "It's all right now, it's over. It is only a dream". It takes a very long time to put that past behind you and to totally forget what happened; I think bits of it will occasionally haunt my dreams and echo in my life forever, despite how well I appear to adapt to life in the outside world.'[1]

A former cult member once described his liberation from the cult as an experience akin to seeing daylight after being imprisoned in a dungeon for many years. Another described it as coming back to planet earth after having been exiled in space.

The 'splashdown' to reality is accompanied by a myriad of feelings and emotions which, although not universal, are common features of the post-cult experience. These feelings and emotions can be deep-seated; resolution can take months and possibly years. However, there are a number of issues which the former cult member must face in the early days after leaving the group.

Submission and Sanity

A primary concern of ex-members is the question of how it was possible to submit to such a group and such an experience. As the former members recover, they recall the activities of the organisation, their blind faith and willingness to participate in numerous illegal activities and immoral acts. Members question their sanity and state of mental and emotional health, wondering whether they will ever be able to rebuild their lives.

One former cult member likened the immediate post-cult experience to waking up after a nightmare. A nightmare represents a set of contradictions in a seemingly normal setting. It is only after one wakes up that one recognises the contradictions and begins to question how it was possible to have accepted them without asking any questions. So, too, being released from a cult is akin to waking up from a nightmare: the contradictions suddenly become painfully obvious and one wonders how it was possible to accept them unquestioningly.

Shame and Guilt

It doesn't take long for former members to recognise the mental and emotional anguish they have caused their family and friends to suffer. They are ashamed of the dishonesty and deception they have practised and the fact that they introduced others to the cult. The cult may have been responsible for the break-up of their marriage and the alienation of their children. Whereas there may be the possibility of reconciliation with the children, the same cannot always be said of the marriage. There have been situations where the former partner has remarried, which only adds to the complexities of the situation.

The guilt is magnified by the person's awareness that though they are now free of the cult's clutches, the people they have introduced are still ensnared.

ANGER AND RESENTMENT

Although it may take time to develop, it is inevitable that former members will begin to express their anger about the cult experience. As they realise the immense waste of opportunity and the gravity of the negative effects of the cult experience, they may seek retribution. As impractical as this may be, it is necessary for them to deal with these emotions and find ways of channelling this anger and rage. This is an ongoing experience. I have found that it can take years for such feelings to be expressed, understood and internalised.

CONFUSION AND DOUBT

Despite all the evidence and the experience of exit counselling, as well as the support now enjoyed, there are moments of doubt. *Maybe the cult was right; maybe this is a test and maybe I'm failing.* The conflict between a mind which is slowly becoming stronger and a heart which is still drawn to the movement can be excruciatingly painful. One former member asked, 'How do I know that the faith I have in my counsellors is no better than the faith I put in my former leaders?'

FEAR

The cult has planted a deep sense of fear in the former member: 'If you leave, you will die. You will never marry and you will be childless.' It is as if a string of curses has been unloaded onto the member. In addition, there is the fear of retribution, the threats of the destruction of family and interference in the workplace.

One of the most tragic experiences I recall concerned two people involved in a Christian cult. Two friends had approached me regarding the possibility of an intervention, and we spent many months preparing for the event. We decided to run two separate interventions rather than see both members at the same time. Both were very difficult, but successful. Following the second intervention, the former member was killed instantly in a car accident. It was a terrible tragedy. Although the boy was an only child, the parents were able to find some comfort in the fact that he had died a free man and not a member of a cult. The cult, on the other hand, was quick to point out the 'dangerous consequences' of deviating from its path.

LACK OF MEANING AND PURPOSE

For better or for worse, the cult experience provided a purpose in life and a sense of meaning. Without it, the individual feels aimless and lost. It is not a simple matter of going back to a former belief system if one did exist. The cult experience has shaken the most basic rudiments of spirituality and the ramifications are far-reaching.

'Ex-members often describe their cult experience as spiritual rape. It can be likened to falling totally in love, changing and conforming yourself so as to merge with your loved one, giving up everything to love and to serve, only to be betrayed. The wound is very deep and will take time to heal.'[2]

A word of warning for counsellors, family and friends. It is both morally wrong and dangerous to be suggesting any replacement philosophy or religion. It is wrong to capitalise on the former cult member's vulnerability by offering an alternative belief system, even if that system is quite genuine and acceptable.

I recall working on an intervention in northern Australia. My team included an ex-member of an Eastern group and of several other organisations. The woman had written a book in which she had documented her experiences — whilst in India, in particular. At the end of the intervention, she presented me with a copy of the book, commenting that she 'hadn't removed the last chapter'. She explained that following involvement in India and her return to Australia, she had been introduced to a woman through whom she had come to embrace Christianity. The woman interpreted her cult experience as an act of God through which she had eventually found her Christian roots. And this was the contents of the last chapter. As she came to terms with her cult experience, she realised that the introduction to any religion on her return to Australia was most inappropriate and she resented the fact that she had written the chapter about 'coming home to God'. She was extremely vulnerable from the effects of her cult involvement.

It is interesting to observe former members and their choices regarding religion or spirituality. Some former members move right away from any religious experience, virtually becoming atheists. Some continue their idealistic pursuits by becoming involved in non-sectarian charity work. Others do move towards religion or other forms of spirituality. Of course, their experiences have taught them to be careful, and it is not uncommon for former members to be very wary as they recommence their search.

A DESIRE TO HELP CULT MEMBERS

This is unfortunately a desire which cannot be fulfilled, at least in the early days after having left a cult. It is no different from running out of a burning house and being advised about the futility and risk to life of returning to save another person. Former members must appreciate that they do not have the resources or strength to be involved with anyone else but themselves. As selfish as it may sound, there are no options, and any attempts to try to 'go back in' will be self-defeating. This awareness and possible accompanying guilt about the fate of others is another burden which the former member must deal with.

In general, former cult members have likened the healing process to recovery after a major operation. Although the progress can be painfully slow, each day brings something new, narrowing the gap between the original experience and the future ahead. This is a difficult process; quite apart from the resolution of personal aspects of recovery, there are issues which are relevant to the family and broader community. This is the topic of our next chapter.

CHAPTER 28

INTEGRATION — RELATING TO THE COMMUNITY

'What do you do when you've been on another planet for up to 20 years or more and you've just returned home? You feel like Rip Van Winkle. Everyone you know, if there are any even still around, is older and at a different place in life. Family and friends are often further along in their education and or/career. They may be married, divorced, own a home or run a business. Not only may you feel like a freak for having been in a cult, but you may feel inadequate when looking at the accomplishments of an old chum.'[1]

As the former cult members commence the difficult task of re-integrating into family and society, they face a number of important issues. Some of them are relevant the moment they leave the cult; others may take some time.

Re-entering the community means re-establishing relationships and creating friendships. For the former cult member, the notion of trust is all but lost, and the process of rebuilding and re-establishing it can take months or years. It is not only a question of trust in another person; trusting oneself is also a new experience. The betrayal that the former cult member feels has rocked the foundation of natural trust and faith in another person. Suspicion of others, especially people who are friendly and warm, is a reflection of the cult experience. Ironically, the more genuinely well-meaning people extend their hand in friendship, the more the former member questions their agenda.

The result of these dilemmas is that it becomes difficult to integrate into the community, further exacerbating the loneliness the former member feels. This experience contrasts starkly to the time spent in the cult, when the member was hardly ever alone. It can be difficult also to dissociate from the cult, and it is not uncommon to feel that 'the world is staring at me'.

Despite the fact that it will take time to re-establish earlier friendships and to find appropriate social networks, the sooner the former member tries, the better. Those who have been involved in serious road accidents are advised to start driving again as soon as possible. Similarly, if someone has been involved in a 'cult accident', it is important to make the effort and take the time to establish appropriate networks.

It would be wonderful if any personal problems which existed prior to the cult experience would have evaporated by the time the person leaves. Perhaps such a development could be seen as compensation for the trauma suffered while in the cult. Unfortunately, life is not so kind, and the reality is that, after his release from the cult, the person may return to the very same circumstances which were responsible, at least in part, for the initial involvement.

I use the words 'may return' deliberately. If the family has worked with the exit counsellor, if the members have sought outside help and done their research, the chances are that the circumstances have changed, and there may be a better opportunity of accommodating their loved one. If the family has not pursued those paths, the situation can be more pressing on the former member.

One person who had been in a cult for almost fifteen years said that he felt like a forty-year-old person in a twenty-five-year-old body. As far as he was concerned, his emotional development had stopped the day he entered the group. And now it was time to make up for what would have been the most productive fifteen years of his life.

Perhaps one of the more trying aspects of cult recovery is the establishment of an appropriate support network with a balanced mix of both lay and professional people. In so far as the professional component is concerned, it is important to determine the nature and frequency of the counselling which will best serve the person.

As far as the lay network is concerned, I have always maintained that the most effective network is small rather than big. A few trusted friends are worth more than a stadium of admirers and supporters. Choose your friends wisely, as they are going to be of tremendous help! But ensure you are able to discuss your experience with them. Don't be afraid of asking a friend whether he is comfortable with your situation; give him the chance to say *no*!

Integration into the community is a slow process; there are no shortcuts. My experience is that, despite the difficulties, over 75 per cent of people successfully re-integrate into the community within a two-year period. I believe that these statistics would be higher if families would participate in counselling both prior to and following an intervention.

Quite apart from the intrinsic value of counselling for the family, the very fact that parents and siblings have agreed to participate in counselling sends the very relevant and powerful message to the former members that the cult experience is a family issue and calls for attention from all members of the family. Shifting the 'blame' from the individual and sharing the responsibility for rehabilitation and recovery sends a welcome message, which diminishes the former members' isolation, their sense of guilt and responsibility.

The pace of family and community integration must be dictated by the former members and not the many well-intentioned people who are trying to assist. The view that the former member should seek employment at once, or study, or became involved with community work, is misguided and dangerous. It can take months to regain the ability to concentrate or study. The establishment of a personal routine is difficult. In the cult, the individuals were regimented and controlled; now they have free choice and mastery over their destiny. They need time and space in order to adjust to this new reality.

CHAPTER 29

MARRIAGE, PERSONAL RELATIONSHIPS, DATING AND SEX

'Don't rush into marriage after you leave a cult. You will feel lonely and overwhelmed at times and you will want the closeness of another person both physically and emotionally. But please remember you have been through a very difficult experience. Give yourself time to heal before you take on new responsibilities. Get to know yourself again (or for the first time) before becoming too involved with another person. This will help you choose the best partner for you.'[1]

The issues of marriage, personal relationships, dating and sex are very significantly affected by the cult experience. Most cults will have regulated their members' sexual values and behaviours. The concept of sex within a relationship may have been reframed; in some cults it is restricted and even prohibited, whilst in others it is encouraged.

Hare Krishna preaches a very restricted code of sexual practice, allowing couples to have sex only once a month and, even then, only under certain conditions. Some of the Christian fundamentalist cults also extol the notion of abstinence or restrictive activity. On the other hand, groups such as Rajneesh and The Children of God are far more liberal in their attitudes, encouraging a relaxed standard of sexual practices. In the past, The Children of God have encouraged the use of sex as a means to recruit new members. In Rajneesh, sex is viewed as the first step towards enlightenment. Bhagwan Rajneesh, the former guru of the organisation, also recommended a twenty-year mandatory period for total birth control, arguing that it was the only way to solve the problem of world overpopulation.

The status of the former member is important in evaluating the impact on her/him of the sexual practices of the group. The challenges are different for the single person, the married or the de facto couple, as well as the situation where one partner has remained in the cult.

For the single person, the post-cult experience and change of environment present the challenge of normal sexual functioning. Some members report that residual innate fears can interfere with intimacy, whilst others have become very adventurous in wanting to prove their ability to function normally. Professor Singer points out that in cults, relationships become sexually neutral and non-threatening.[2]

Unrealistic expectations and the need for security should not facilitate premature attempts to enter into a relationship. Recovery needs to be well under way before anything serious can be considered. At the same time, it is important to recognise that the revitalisation of this significant area of our lives and psyche marks a major step in personal fulfilment and community integration.

It is also possible that individuals — or for that matter couples — were experiencing difficulties in relation to intimacy prior to entering the cult. For some people, the restrictive sexual practices of the cult may even have been an attraction, because they made it possible to avoid dealing with their problems. The chances are that these problems still exist; they may even have been magnified. So it is important that the person or couple seek help to resolve these issues.

For the married or de facto couple who have left the cult, there are other challenges. In the situation where the sexual relationship was dominated by the cult doctrine as well as numerous rituals and practices, the couple may need assistance in re-establishing normal sexual interaction. In that respect, the sexual relationship may act as a trigger for the cult imagery to create anxiety and dysfunction. Psychotherapy is an option that couples should consider in this situation. The problem can be resolved. It is a question of what means the couple will use in order to solve it.

The plight of the person whose partner remains in the cult is a very difficult one. One of the issues relates to the question of loyalties and expectations. How long one should wait before considering an alternative relationship? Although this alternative is not relevant during the post-cult period, which may last for a year or more, it does come into focus once things have settled down and there is the opportunity to review personal options. We are talking here of a very specific problem, and I can only advise individuals in that predicament to seek professional help from people who understand the cult scene. This assistance is also valuable in helping the non-cult members develop strategies regarding communication with their partners. There may also be legal implications which require attention.

The couple who were married in the cult on the orders of the guru face a different set of problems. The question is whether the marriage will survive beyond the cult experience in the event of both partners leaving. Many of these marriages are total mismatches, which have been held together by the cult doctrine and the leader's wishes. Once these factors have been taken out of the relationship, there is a strong possibility that it will not last.

A couple who had been married in a Moonie marriage approached me for assistance after they had both successfully left the group. Their relationship had developed since the day they met each other for the first time at the mass marriage ceremony. They were prepared to keep working at it. However, they were finding the process particularly difficult because they felt that by remaining married, they were fulfilling the wishes of Rev. Moon.

This couple had managed to leave the Moonies on their own. However, the absence of any exit counselling had left them confused and unsure about how to deal with their former cult experience. They were making the mistake of thinking that whatever had happened as a result of their being in a cult was bad. They were relieved to hear that this was not the case and that there was nothing wrong with recognising any good which may have been generated by the group, regardless of the fact that the group itself was corrupt or destructive.

Because issues of sexuality and intimacy are so closely connected with the soul and the psyche, it is understandable that in these areas the cults' damage can be significant. It can take years to recover from the invasion of privacy and prostitution of values. As a former member put it to me, 'The wounds will heal, but the scars will always remain.' The situation becomes even more tragic when the result of the cult influence is irreversible, such as the case of sterilisation, condemning the former members to a lifelong sentence and depriving them of the greatest human gift.

I have found that the resumption of normal personal relationships is one of the greatest challenges confronting the former member. If mishandled, without appropriate guidance, it can lead to a major downfall and a renewed sense of personal defeat. But if the former members are able to build on their earlier experiences, including life in the cult, the re-creation of meaningful and loving relationships can bring the greatest rewards and comfort — in a sense, the most significant form of compensation for the destructive cult experience.

CHAPTER 30

WHAT ABOUT THE CHILDREN?

'Why did we hate ourselves even when we were only little kids? I think it was because we had been so successfully indoctrinated with the idea that we were terribly unworthy. If you are told incessantly that you are horrible, that you are ugly, fat, stupid and inferior, you start to believe it. As a child you know no other truth than that which you are taught by those around you.

'Perhaps too, we wanted to hurt ourselves because it didn't feel right unless we were being punished for something. It somehow felt better that we were hurting. In a strange sort of way that offered comfort. Maybe it was because the only form of human contact we knew was physical abuse. Even if it hurt it was interaction and attention and human touch; all the things that children need and crave.'[1]

The majority of cases I have dealt with have involved the adult population. The ages of the people concerned have ranged from the late teens up to the fifties and even sixties. Other exit counsellors report working with older people as well.

There is another group of people who deserve attention, whose post-cult symptoms are, in certain ways, more serious than those of the adult population. This innocent and defenceless group has grown up in the cult environment, having been born into the group or having become involved at a very early age. These are the children of cults.

Earlier chapters referred to the cult's influence in creating a pseudo-personality or dual identity. This suggests that, regardless of the strength of the cult influence, the original identity of the cult member remains intact, buried deep beneath the environment, the pressure and the influence of the cult experience. Exit counselling is essentially a means by which the cult member is put back in touch and reconnected with that original person. But the children who are either born into the movement or become involved early in their life have not yet had the chance to develop their own identities. They have no social experience and have not yet established a relationship with the world. They may have been denied the normal social interaction with other children and in all probability have been reared in an environment that demands total obedience and discourages critical thinking.

Such children have been brought up by people who label the outside world as evil. They have been taught to avoid contact with non-cult members at all costs: contact is dangerous and may bring them harm. Whereas in the outside environment, children are brought up to watch before they cross the road, stay away from dangerous pets and avoid talking to strangers, the cult children may be taught to stay away from their extended family and avoid talking to anyone without permission.

In the case of the Hamilton-Byrne cult in Victoria, the officer investigating the group asked the children their names. Their responses included their full names as well as their dates of birth. These children had been programmed to respond to outsiders in a particular way. The encounter with the officer may have been their first test of that training.

Most cults develop an anxious, dependent personality.[2] Exit counselling assists the adult to reduce the levels of anxiety and dependency. This is not necessarily the case with children, as these traits may have become an integral part of their personality. Whereas adults have the ability to look objectively at the fears and phobias which the cult has implanted in them and judge them against their pre-cult experiences, children have no prior life experience against which to judge the cult.

Children freed from cults are likely to experience difficulties in adjusting to any form of authority, whether emanating from parents or from an educational setting. The development of social skills, trust in peers and tolerance of other lifestyles will take time and, in general, will be assisted by appropriate forms of therapy. As has been pointed out in relation to former adult members, it will be necessary for therapists to be familiar with the cult process in order to work effectively with their clients. Once again the issue of education becomes relevant.

There are many different situations which may involve former cult members who are children. If a whole family was removed from a cult, the situation will, at least in its formative stages, be complicated by the fact that the parents are also involved in the recovery process, which is emotionally draining and time-consuming.

If friends or the extended family of children involved in a cult manage to rescue them from the group or if the authorities do, the children will require fostering, either short-term, until they are joined by their parent/s, or long-term if the chances of the parent/s leaving the group are very remote.

Another situation arises when a non-cult parent has successfully managed to gain custody of his 'cult-child'. In both this case and the previous one, the situation is seriously exacerbated by the issue of separation from the cult-parent/s. My experience with this type of scenario is limited. Nevertheless, the few situations in which I have been involved have been complex and disturbing. It is difficult to imagine the feelings and desperation of a child who has effectively lost his/her cult parent/s, been removed from a familiar environment and forced to live with 'evil people'.

One final point in relation to the situation where the involvement of a cult member extends to children or where children are being sent overseas to schools run by the cults: these situations must be looked at very seriously. Because of the potential extent of the harm to children in the destructive cult milieu, it may be necessary to pressure child protection authorities to intervene. Unfortunately, many of these government institutions work very slowly, and considerable pressure may need to be exerted on the relevant authority to achieve results. Where this is necessary, it is advisable to involve cult experts who can inform this authority about the risks of continuing cult involvement and help devise a plan to resolve the problem. I have already documented several examples where a government's ignorance has led to unco-ordinated and inappropriate responses to cult situations.

Considering that so many young people joined cults in the past ten to fifteen years, the cult problem is certain to become more prominent as they grow up and have children. The call for further education and professional training with which to deal with these tragic situations should be treated as a matter of urgency.

CHAPTER 31

AFTER THE CULT — THE FAMILY

'It's hard when a friend or family member who was close to you now is physically and emotionally distant. He is alone with his pain and you can't reach him ... Like a veteran returning from war, he has been somewhere you haven't been, exposed to horrors of a trauma you can only imagine. For all your years of experience, you have not been in this war. You did not lose the time, friends, and dreams that he lost. But you still lost something. You lost your loved one the way he used to be. He is back but he will never be who he was.'[1]

As traumatic as it is for the former member to leave a cult, it is also very difficult for the family to know how to welcome back this loved one. The exit counselling preparation will have given the family an insight into some of the challenges they face as they begin to readjust to the presence of a member who may have been involved in a cult for many years.

Various issues are worthy of discussion. One primary issue is the potential effect the cult experience may have on the parents. Particular problems, past conflicts or marital discord may be exacerbated as a result of the cult experience of a son or daughter. The possibility of one parent blaming the other can be compounded by the amount of time spent with the former cult member, sometimes at the expense of the marital relationship. Parents may feel a sense of shame and failure, as well as hopelessness and rejection because of the cult involvement.

The parents may have to face the reality that their loved one has lost the opportunity for studies or career or that s/he will remain stigmatised by the cult experience. It is not easy to accept the changes brought about by the cult and to let go of expectations and hopes which may never again be fulfilled.

There may be added financial responsibilities on the family as it endeavours to support the former member, although this support should be seen as a temporary measure, only a stepping-stone on the road towards financial independence. At the same time, siblings may resent the amount of time the parents are spending with their brother or sister. One teenager once said to me, 'First she [the cult member] destroys the family by disappearing for two years. Now she's back, and everyone else might as well disappear.' The balancing act is not easy.

Meanwhile there are numerous skills the parents must learn in order to remain a positive influence within the renewed family structure.

They will need to adjust to the transition from parenting a younger child — when they made decisions, provided support as well as food, shelter and money — to forming an adult relationship with their loved one. They must learn to be good listeners, making suggestions if asked and not being 'over-helpful' if not required. Being over-protective or controlling doesn't help. Independent decision-making should be encouraged.

Even though parents will view the cult involvement of their loved one as counter-productive and destructive, they need to recognise the strengths gained from the experience: the effort and energy that went into the rigid cult discipline, the loyalty to the leader and any study that took place. Once the person is out of the movement, these practices can, in hindsight, be transformed into powerful learning experiences.

At the same time, parents must understand that it can take time to let go of the feelings of loyalty to the group and its leaders and to acknowledge fully the deception they orchestrated.

Parents will be uncomfortable if the person has contact with members who are still in the cult. Although this is a genuine concern, the matter needs to be discussed, so that there is no apparent effort to undermine the former member's autonomy or sense of competence.

Leaving a cult can be accompanied by emotional reactions, including loss, grief and anger. Family members, in their attempts to be supportive, can be overly intrusive, continually asking, 'What's wrong?' A delicate balance is required between the parents' willingness to listen and respect for the person's privacy and space. Parents may offer opportunities to join in particular activities, but they must accept that the invitation may be declined.[2]

Former members talk about the need for forgiveness as well as confirmation of the fact that the parents still love them. It is not enough for the family to assume that these messages are being transmitted. Wendy Ford adds a salient point when she says that cult members need to forgive themselves.[3]

Parents may have kept secret the fact that their child was involved in a cult. It must be left to the son or daughter to decide whom to talk to and to tell about the experience. Parents will require guidance from their loved one in regard to telling their own friends and peers. I recall a situation where a former member was very aggrieved by the fact that his family was playing down his cult experience. He wanted his close relatives to know the truth about what he had suffered whilst in the group and to recognise the efforts he was making during recovery. Instead he felt that denial, which had been an early feature of his parents' response to his joining the cult had returned.

There is no 'fast forward' when it comes to recovery, and it is counter-productive to compare notes with other former members. The rate of a recovery is an individual matter, and parents need to understand that recovery may take years. It may be necessary for them to seek counselling with an appropriate therapist in order to come to terms with these issues. Apart from its own intrinsic value, it sends their loved one the message that the parents regard the cult problem as a family issue.

'As you act in a non-threatening and nurturing way, you are building a bridge for ex-cultists from the world they left behind to a new place. The stronger this bridge is to the new world, the easier the transition is away from the old one. You are competing with an illusion of total acceptance and love. You have one thing the illusion doesn't have though. You have integrity.'[4]

PART 8

EXIT COUNSELLING IS NOT ALWAYS THE ANSWER

- BUT WE CAN'T DO IT!

- WHAT TO DO IF THE EXIT COUNSELLING DOESN'T WORK

- OTHER REASONS NOT TO GO AHEAD

I try to explain to clients that working with cult victims is often very much a roller-coaster ride. There are moments when everything looks just right; there are times when things appear to come to a grinding halt.

The changes are not necessarily related to the cult victims and their circumstances. The concerned family also has its own agenda, and numerous issues may affect its ability to proceed with an intervention. Within that setting, I am often faced with the painful decision of whether or not to go ahead.

The family response to a decision to abandon the intervention, at least for the time being, can be quite revealing. The responses range from a sense of temporary relief to anxiety at the thought of the cult victim continuing his involvement in the group.

My task is to explain to the family that it is very common to put plans on hold, and that such a decision is part of a longer-term process. There will be other more appropriate opportunities; yes, it is just a matter of waiting until they arise.

Families are concerned about the work that has gone into preparation: what about the hours and days of discussions and meetings, of raised hopes and expectations?

Unfortunately, those concerns often override the benefits that have been derived from the process, which include a renewed awareness on the part of the family of the plight of their loved one. The family has pooled its emotional and intellectual resources to find a solution, and its efforts represent a statement that it will not abandon the particular person but will continue to work towards the restoration of that person's freedom and independence.

I am fascinated by the revelations of former cult members who are able to identify the actual time when the family became involved in the preparation for the intervention which finally freed them. From those very early days, they perceived changes in their family and the reaction of family members towards them. In hindsight, they are able to recognise increased levels of tolerance and even warmth.

Preparation for an intervention is rarely a waste of time. It is part of a process, the beginning of a journey. Sometimes the journey just takes a little longer.

CHAPTER 32

BUT WE CAN'T DO IT!

'To leave a cult like this takes massive courage. On Anne's orders these people had cut ties with their families unless they too were cult members. Their social and professional circles consisted of cult people. If cult members showed any kind of doubt, they were persecuted by everyone they knew ... so it was in their interests to stay safe and silent within the bosom of The Family.'[1]

The initial meetings have taken place, the family has read the books and even met the exit counsellors. However, the intervention is not on. Perhaps the reason is that the family has not been able to come to terms with the idea or that there appears no realistic plan in place to bring the cult member to participate. The timing or the cost may be an issue as well. The family may feel that the cult member is not ready for an intervention or lacks the courage actually to leave the group.

It is not unusual for families to back out, even at the last minute. At Cult Counselling Australia we are conscious of this possibility. When we use overseas exit counsellors, we have them call us from the airport prior to departure to ensure that the intervention is still going ahead.

As mentioned earlier, we are not prepared to attempt to influence families about their final decision. Our task is to provide as much information as is available, as well as support to the families. Ultimately, the decision to go ahead or not is their own. If they decline, we make it clear that in the event of a change of heart, there will always be another opportunity.

Just as going ahead is difficult, so too is the decision not to. This decision is often accompanied with feelings of guilt and neglected responsibility. It is important to reassure families about the importance of making a decision which they feel is justified and with which they are comfortable.

However, it is a mistake to suggest that a decision not to go ahead with an intervention should be regarded as justification for doing nothing regarding the problem they are facing. Not going ahead with the intervention simply means that there will be no active plan involving third persons to extricate the cult member from the cult environment.

There are numerous other options the family retains in the face of this decision. Not only is their implementation a means by which the guilt issue can be resolved, but they may pave the way for an improved relationship with the cult member and maybe even a voluntary exit.

First and foremost, families must ensure that they remain in contact with their loved ones. Putting aside the question as to whether mail actually reaches its destination, it is important to write regularly, even if there are no responses. The content of any letters should include a clear message of love and care for the cult member, as well as the hope that there will be opportunities to meet and to talk. There is no place for condemnation or attack in these letters — it would only create greater alienation. Families should note that there is every possibility the letter is being read by the cult authorities well before it reaches its destination and should be written with that in mind.

Regardless of the chances of a favourable outcome, friends of the cult member should be encouraged to visit the person and retain contact. If the person is unavailable, they should not hesitate to question the cult authorities and to make it known they find it strange that the person they wish to see is always inaccessible. If entry is still refused, they can leave a note. Friends and relatives should not be discouraged by the lack of response from the cult member. They should continue to visit, regardless of the outcome. The isolation cult members experience is a powerful tool in strengthening their dependence on the group.

Whilst cults attempt to restrict contact by family and friends, they also capitalise on the issue by asking the member why nobody has bothered to inquire about their welfare. As contrived as it is, the cults use this in order to reinforce the distance from family and friends and strengthen the conviction that 'only we care'. I advise parents to keep copies of all their correspondence so that if the person leaves, they can compare what was written and sent to what was actually received. The fact that the cult withheld or censored the mail could certainly be useful information at a later time.

Families should continue to learn more about cults and the particular group which is relevant to their predicament. If they feel comfortable with the idea, parents may attend the church or the organisation's premises to observe a prayer session or participate in a lecture. In some situations it may be advisable not to attempt to speak to the cult member; better for the member to be curious as to why they attended. The member then has to decide whether to approach them.

Use of the media is always an option, although I generally discourage it and use it only as a last resort. However, if the family has decided not to go ahead with an intervention, they can look more closely at the media option. Most media groups will not publish a story unless the person who has brought it to their attention is prepared to identify themself, and this could have serious implications in terms of further alienation. But sometimes an anonymous tip-off to the media about the activities of a cult can provoke interest which may work in favour of the family.

Unlike the cults, which have been described as being very 'black-and-white', the choices confronting families are far more subtle. What suits the family may not suit the cult member. What suits the cult member may not be practical for the family at that time. The answer is not necessarily a decision to go ahead with an intervention. There are so many other options, which may be less decisive but nevertheless eventually help in achieving the family's aims.

I have always believed that parents should trust their own intuition. In the face of interventions that failed, I have empathised with those who have admitted later on, 'We knew all along that it didn't feel right.' Sometimes, that intuition and those sentiments can be more valuable than the facts, the figures and the statistics. Don't be afraid to trust yourself!

CHAPTER 33

WHAT TO DO IF THE EXIT COUNSELLING DOESN'T WORK

'Parents will be immensely discouraged and sad if their child decides not to leave the group, but even so, an effective intervention will actually enhance communication and restore bonds with the family. When these bonds are intact and strong, the family member will not feel threatened to talk to parents when they later grow disillusioned with the cult. Any intervention that enhances communication is a success.'[1]

The issue of success has been discussed in an earlier chapter. Although, ideally, the result of an intervention would see the cult member sever ties with the group, this is not always the case. The benefits of the exit counselling process will hopefully include better family communication as well as improved understanding of cultism and the effect it is having on the member. The member has absorbed a significant amount of information as well as felt family love and support; the family will not give up on attempts to be reunited. In addition, the way may have been laid for a future intervention.

Nevertheless, the reality is that the family has invested heavily in this intervention. They have spent months researching the group, investigating their options, interviewing exit counsellors and developing strategies. It can be painful when the end result is that the member remains in the cult.

The person may have walked away from the intervention. They may have stayed until the end, requested a few days to think it over, and then rejoined the movement. They may have actually left, only to return to the group as a result of 'floating'. There are many ways in which a cult member returns to the group.

Regardless of all the preparation and the emphasis on 'no guarantees', it is difficult to prepare a family for 'failure'. The realisation that the intervention has not worked can be devastating. In that event the family requires support and encouragement.

There are two primary areas of concern when the cult member decides to return to a group. The first relates to the interaction between the exit counsellors and the member before they leave. The second relates to the responsibility of the family both prior to the member's departure and afterwards.

Exit counsellors are trained to discern the progress of the intervention. The family's assessment of the progress is often influenced by their own agenda, emotive issues as well as expectations. In Michael's situation, there were times when his family was quite worried, yet the exit counsellors were satisfied with the progress. The exit counsellors are trained to be able to detect any desire on the part of the cult member to walk out of the intervention.

This is particularly important in giving them the opportunity to talk to the cult member before this happens. That discussion is crucial. If the cult member walks out without a final discussion or briefing, some of the benefits of the intervention may be lost.

In her highly recommended book *Exit Counselling, A Family Intervention*,[2] Carol Giambalvo addresses the role of the exit counsellors when it is clear that the cult member will be returning to the group. She suggests they remind the cult member that the purpose of the intervention was twofold, in that it provided information not readily available to the individual through the group as well as information about mind control and undue influence. 'The exit counsellors should reinforce the good intentions and motivation of the family, underlining the fact that everything is now out in the open. Always encourage future communication.'

The client should be prepared for the likelihood that for a short time the group may hold the member up as a hero, but they might also distort what actually happened in the intervention. 'The exit counsellors should ask what *actually* happened and the way he or she was actually treated. Remind the client of the importance of keeping his or her own integrity intact.'

And lastly, Giambalvo suggests that, if possible, the exit counsellors should role-play how the member thinks the leaders will handle the return to the group and how the member will respond to questioning as to why they weren't called for advice when faced with the intervention.

The second area of responsibility lies with the family. Prior to their loved one's departure from the intervention, they need to make every effort to speak with the person. It is advisable to include the following in their discussion:

'We want you to know that we love you and that it was only because we love you that we organised this meeting. We have appreciated your willingness to participate in the meeting and to share your views with us.

'We have given you as much information as we were able. We want you to remember these discussions. When you return to your group, try to measure the performance there against the criteria for mind control we have discussed. Although the group will not be happy about this meeting, we hope you will see this as a beginning of improved communication with us.

'We do not regret having organised this meeting and are not angry at you for deciding to return to the group. This has been a difficult time for all of us, but it has been worth while.'

At that point the family may discuss ways in which the communication may be improved. It may be worth noting down the suggestions to see if they are actually followed through.

Finally, it is certainly worth while to ask the loved one if there is anything they would like to say. A response may be very useful in determining how effective the intervention has been and what impression it has made.

Following the intervention, the family should attempt to maintain the level of communication through whatever means possible, including phone calls, letters and visits. Various means by which the family can stay in touch are discussed in the previous chapter. Unless complete privacy is assured, the intervention should not be mentioned during these communications. However, where privacy permits, it is worth while for the family to continue to reinforce the points made at the end of the intervention.

One further point. There is a popular belief that 'you only get one shot at an intervention'. Not true. Although a break is required before a second attempt can be made, I have seen numerous interventions work on a second attempt. Such an effort can be more difficult, however, because the member has her/his defences up and may have received special instructions from the cult on how to counteract any attempt to remove her/him from the group.

Quite clearly, the decision of a cult member to return to the group can be problematic for the family. Their ability to cope with the situation will depend on the preparation done for the intervention. If, for example, the family maintained complete confidentiality, the difficulty is avoided of explaining to friends and relatives what happened or 'what went wrong'. If the family understood the various ways of defining success, it will be easier to come to terms with the outcome of the intervention — which is the first step towards the next attempt.

CHAPTER 34

OTHER REASONS NOT
TO GO AHEAD

'We have both good news and bad news. Anthony did finally leave the group. However, shortly afterwards, he attempted to take his life and is currently in hospital. We are grateful for all your assistance, in particular the advice not to go ahead with an intervention considering that Anthony's state of mind was very fragile. We are confident that he will recover and not return. We will keep you informed.'

As we have said, it is not always possible to go ahead with an intervention. It is important to identify the situations where this is the case and to ensure that the family understands the issues involved.

Mental health has already been mentioned. The orientation meeting presents an opportunity for the family to discuss this issue with a cult expert. Where the cult member has a mental health problem, it may be advisable to defer the intervention until such time as a mental health professional has assessed the situation. The circumstances which would require such a consultation are varied.

If the cult member has shown any suicidal or self-destructive tendencies, the intervention has the potential to exacerbate this condition. Although exit counselling is essentially an opportunity for the various parties to exchange information, the impact on the cult members is significant, as their belief system and glorification of the leader are challenged. Former members have described the situation as painful, even torturous. If there has been a previous pattern of self-destructive or suicidal behaviour, the possibility exists that the member will respond to the situation by harming themself.

Similarly, where a member has a record of violent behaviour, it is not possible to place the family and the exit counsellors at risk through an intervention. If the member has had a psychotic episode, it is vital for a mental health professional to determine the risk factor in conducting the intervention.

There are numerous other circumstances which demand attention, including eating disorders, depression, obsessive-compulsive behaviour. In these circumstances it may be possible to go ahead with the intervention, but the exit counselling team might be advised to have psychiatric back-up.

These assessments are very difficult, because in most instances at the time of the orientation meeting the mental health professional will not have access to the cult member and will have to rely on previous records, which may be quite dated. There is also the possibility of a problematic physical condition. Whether it be pregnancy or an illness such as diabetes, or an anaemic condition, a medical practitioner will be required to advise the team. Whenever stress may exacerbate an existing condition, the family must be careful.

Parents' circumstances may prevent the intervention from going ahead. If the parents are in the midst of a separation or divorce or if they have just experienced a traumatic event, the intervention may need to be put on hold. If they show signs of instability or if one or both have a drug or alcohol problem, the intervention cannot go ahead.

In general, it is advisable for the exit counsellors to have access to a medical practitioner or psychiatrist if advice is needed during the intervention. The professional should have a knowledge of cultism as well as an understanding of the exit counselling process.

In relation to mental health issues, parents are often quick to point out that the situation has changed and the risks are no longer present. My own practice is to rely on the last available information, regardless of the fact that the situation may have changed. This can be difficult for families to accept. Two points are relevant:

Firstly, I explain to them that by going ahead with the intervention, they could be placing their loved one at risk. A fragile or disturbed person may respond to the intervention in a manner harmful to them. Suicides are irreversible. So too are miscarriages.

Secondly, I point out that, in my experience, a significant percentage of cult members with mental health problems have either left the group or been thrown out. In one sense this information may not be very comforting; in another, it does suggest that the term of the member's involvement may be limited. However, parents need to be aware that if the member leaves, it may be necessary to provide exit counselling and substantial support.

Quite apart from the mental health issue, there may be any number of practical problems preventing the intervention from going ahead. They may include cost factors, or difficulty of obtaining appropriate exit counsellors or a facilitator for the intervention.

And finally, an intervention may need to be put on hold because the family doesn't feel the timing is right or because they haven't reached total agreement on the actual process. Whichever the case, it is advisable to delay until these issues are totally resolved.

Understandably, it may be difficult for anxious and concerned parents to accept the fact that the intervention must be put on hold. It is important for the family to understand the reasons so that they are able to look forward to a time when it may be practical to resume the process. As has been pointed out, there are numerous steps the family can take during that interim period. The family's willingness to follow these steps and to retain communication with their loved one is the key to future success.

CHAPTER 35

GOVERNMENTS AND LAWMAKERS CAN NO LONGER SIT STILL

'"Freedom of religion" is not freedom, for example, to defraud, nor is it freedom to cause significant psychological or psychiatric harm to any person.'[1]

The cult issue remains controversial because it touches on the basic and democratic right of freedom of religion. Any attempts to curtail the operation of a 'religious group' are bound to attract criticism from civil liberty organisations as well as from a wary public concerned about the misuse of public control.

Ironically, in response to any form of curtailment of their activities, the cults accuse the authorities of intolerance and religious vilification. Exit counsellors are accused of brainwashing their clients and denying them their basic religious rights.

Caught in the middle is the family who seeks assistance through legal or other means to re-establish contact with their loved one. There appear to be avenues through which to pursue allegations of physical, emotional and sexual abuse. Few options exist in regard to psychological manipulation and abuse.

Although many cults have been accused of breaking the law, any response by the authorities will be limited to the alleged offence. Generally, these offences relate to tax matters, corporate reporting requirements and violation of immigration laws.

There is some assistance for children who are caught up in a cult-based residency conflict, for example, where a former cult member is applying for custody in relation to a child who remains in the cult with the other parent. The former member may be assisted by guidelines set down by the Full Court of the Family Court in 1994, which recognises that situations exist which call for the appointment of a child's representative — where the child's interests require independent representation. They include cases:

- involving allegations of child abuse whether physical, sexual or psychological;
- where the child is apparently alienated from one or both parents;
- where there are real issues of cultural or religious differences affecting the child;
- where the conduct of either or both parents or some other person having significant contact with the child is alleged to be anti-social to the extent that it seriously impinges the child's welfare.[2]

The appointment of a child's representative in a cult-related case could facilitate an assessment of the child's mental state and the influence of the group on her/him. This may lead to a court making specific rulings to protect the child or ultimately remove the child from the cult environment.

The situation is different in relation to adults who do not enjoy that level of protection by virtue of their age and legal status. Police are not able to respond to complaints lodged by parents unless it can be demonstrated that an offence has been committed by the cult. There is very limited recourse for parents who are concerned about the plight of their adult children involved in a cult, regardless of the effect it may be having on them. There may be grounds for legal action by former members against a cult, but such a course could be expensive and traumatic.

In the past few years there have been various attempts to introduce legislation regarding this issue. Of particular note were the attempts in 1993 of a New Zealand MP Nick Smith to introduce legislation regarding the Family Proceedings Act and the way it could be manipulated in custody cases where a child had been turned against one or both parents through undue emotional pressure. Mr Smith was examining the possibility of legislating against inciting or encouraging the break-up of marital relations or of contact between relatives under the guise of religion.

Referring to a particular fringe church, Mr Smith said, 'In the bulk of cases I have no problem with this. But in respect to the Exclusive Brethren and the way they poison the children against the parents outside the church, I think there needs to be a conditional clause. Such a clause would make express the preferential custody rights of the natural parents, as long as they provide no emotional or physical threat to the well-being of the children.'[3]

Unfortunately, Mr Smith's strenuous efforts did not lead to any changes in the Family Proceedings Act.

More recently, an official committee of federal, state and territory governments has recommended that 'significant emotional harm' inflicted by religious groups be classified as a criminal offence. The report cited a California Supreme Court finding that 'coercive persuasion' by religious sects may cause 'serious physical and psychiatric disorders'.[4]

The committee named the techniques used by cults as isolation, manipulation of time and attention, positive and negative reinforcement, peer group pressure, prohibition of dissent, deprivation of sleep and protein and the inducement of fear, guilt and emotional dependence.[5]

Although this development is welcome, it remains to be seen whether it can be implemented. Nevertheless, it is important in that it represents an attempt to make cults accountable for their methods and activities.

The issue of accountability is significant. Despite the difficulties involved in attempting to introduce controls into the booming industry of cults and cult-like personal development groups, the matter deserves urgent attention. Fringe churches assume the mantle of established religious organisations without revealing their true identity or disclosing their long-term agendas. Some personal development groups operate without any form of accreditation, often awarding certificates or diplomas of no recognised academic or professional value. Cults purport to offer salvation and healing to vulnerable and often desperate individuals; exorbitant sums of money are extracted with little or no return to the member. Spiritualists and psychic healers are able to practise without any formal training or external control.

The challenge to governments and lawmakers is to put in place a system of checks and balances whereby these groups are required to conform to a code of ethics under a regulatory board, which can oversee their operation. Failure to do so should attract appropriate penalties as well as the possibility of the organisation being closed down. Despite the controversial nature of the issues involved, such a process is long overdue.

In addition, it is necessary to educate relevant government and non-government personnel regarding cults and their subtle processes of psychological manipulation and mind control. This information is relevant to numerous agencies, including the family courts, departments of community and human services, child abuse and protective agencies, sexual abuse clinics, medical practitioners and counselling services.

Where necessary, agencies must be prepared to call on expert advice in dealing with cult-related matters. Thus, for example, a child's representative appointed by the Family Court should have access to expertise in the cult arena. If necessary, the courts should be empowered to remove the suspected victim from the cult for the purpose of an assessment, as well as to initiate action against the organisation that is acting unethically or corruptly.

To date, the record of governments and lawmakers regarding the cult issue has been mainly reactive. A mass suicide or the disappearance of an individual into a cult tends to mobilise the relevant authorities into suggesting new laws or controls for these groups. But as quickly as these concerns arise, they dissipate. Families and communities deserve better. Australia prides itself on being a tolerant, democratic and free society. If the beneficiaries of this freedom are the destructive cults and the fringe churches, then we have to question the way these principles are being applied in our society.

Epilogue

Back in the 1960s it was difficult to imagine that a few, relatively new Eastern cults would be the forerunners of what has been termed an epidemic of sudden personality change. Even in 1978, the tragedy of Jonestown was regarded as an isolated incident, with remote likelihood of any repetition.

But since then the world has experienced the harsh reality and implications of the cult phenomenon. It is disturbing that the frequency of tragedies is increasing. By focusing on the suicides and the deaths, we overlook the massive human suffering and pain of those who remain in the cults, their families and friends.

There is no reason to believe that the cult problem will go away. The changes within the cult scene indicate the mushrooming of new groups. These new groups, which present a far cleaner and professional image, are no less dangerous than those we learnt about when all this started. It makes detection far more difficult. Families and friends are confused, and the problems continue.

Governments attempt to balance the views of the anti-cult movement against the civil libertarians, which means that cult activity is able to continue unabated. Although most tragedies create an outpouring of emotion and a call for change, as we have noted, these sentiments are usually short-lived. This has certainly been the case in relation to Jonestown, Waco, The Order of the Solar Temple, Heaven's Gate and numerous other tragedies.

The geographical isolation of Australia as well as apathy on the part of our government have enabled numerous cults to establish themselves here. The specific cases highlighted in this book demonstrate a government approach which has been either non-existent or misguided.

In Australia Section 116 of the Constitution and in the USA the First Amendment have provided a safety zone within which the cults can operate, although this was probably *not* the intention of the founding fathers and the authors of the constitutions.[1] Other Western countries offer similar 'cover' through which the cults are given a free hand. There is little reason and even less hope for change in the short term.

The cults are a challenge to society at large, with a particular responsibility on the part of the churches to respond aggressively and effectively. Although it is becoming increasingly clear that the cults are not a religious issue, it is also clear that they offer an opportunity that appears attractive in religious or spiritual terms. Against the backdrop of a growing divorce rate, a spiralling crime rate and community unrest the seductive message of the cults is increasingly convincing, even inspiring.

This message is not restricted to cults alone, but to an expanding range of new philosophies and belief systems. An analysis by Professor Gary Bouma of Monash University in Melbourne found that between 1991 and 1996 the New Age movements in Australia flourished. 'Paganism tripled, nature and earth-based religions grew by 130%, Satanism doubled its numbers and Scientology grew by 50%.'[2]

Ultimately, the cults have exposed the frailty of the human mind and the vulnerability of our psyche. They have shown that we are far from immune to the carefully contrived plans of groups and organisations that well understand the notion of mind control and psychological manipulation. What was once regarded as a phenomenon unique to prisoners of war and hostages is now seen as a major threat to freedom, autonomy and individuality and, ultimately, to our freedom as citizens.

We have learnt very quickly that, under the right conditions, we are vulnerable. A new insight is emerging into the atrocities of Nazi Germany and today's fundamentalist movements, as we compare the techniques used by the Third Reich with those of some of the more extreme cults that we face today. As the excellent film *The Wave* was able to prove, a carefully orchestrated plan of mind control is capable of drawing people to any hate party or philosophy of extermination. When the submission of one human being to another is complete, the leader's word reigns supreme, regardless of the state of mind or the level of deluded thinking. Once that point has been reached, it makes no difference whether the leader directs followers to a new diet, a new mission or mass suicide.

During the course of my research in this field, there was one quote which stood out. It has been cited in numerous books and continues to carry a relevant and inspiring message, which we cannot afford to ignore. If I had my way it would hang as a banner at Los Angeles Airport and in Times Square in New York and on the Sydney Harbour Bridge and the Rialto Tower in Melbourne; it would be included in every human development program in our educational systems:

'When you meet the friendliest people you have ever known, who introduce you to the most loving group you have ever encountered, and you find the leader to be the most inspired, caring, compassionate and understanding person you have ever met, and then you learn the cause of the group is something you never dared hope could be accomplished, and all of this sounds too good to be true — it probably *is* too good to be true! Don't give up your education, your hopes and ambitions to follow a rainbow.'[3]

Endnotes

Introduction

[1]   Konrad Lorenz, quoted in *Australia Israel Review*, May 1978.

[2]   Conway and Siegelman, *Snapping: America's Epidemic of Sudden Personality Change*, Stillpoint Press, New York, 1978; updated 1995, second edition.

Part 1
Chapter 1

[1]   'The Departed Children', *The Province*, Vancouver, 1989.

[2]   Marcia Rudin, 'Cults Not Gone, Just Mainstreaming', *The Cult Observer*, Vol. 10, No. 10, 1993, American Family Foundation, Bonita Springs, USA.

[3]   Definition of channeling: 'Channeling is the communication of information to or through a physically embodied human being from a source that is said to exist on some other level or dimension of reality than the physical as we know it, and that is not from the normal mind (or self) of the channel.' Jon Klimo, *Channeling*, The Aquarian Press, Los Angeles, CA, 1988.

[4]   Dr Michael Car-Gregg, Letter to the Editor, 'The dangers of Love-bombing' *The Age*, 1 April 1997, Melbourne.

Chapter 2

[1]   Sarah Hamilton-Byrne, *Unseen, Unheard, Unknown*, Penguin Books, Melbourne, 1995.

[2]   Michael Langone, 'Introduction', *Recovery from Cults*, W. W. Norton & Co., San Francisco, CA, 1993.

[3]   Robert J. Lifton, 'Cult Formation', *The Harvard Mental Health Letter*, Vol. 7, No. 8, February 1991, Boston, MA.

[4]   *Ibid.*; see also Margaret Singer, with Janja Lalich, *Cults in Our Midst*, Jossey-Boss, San Francisco, CA, 1996.

5   Cate Brett, 'History of the Exclusive Brethren', *North South*, New Zealand, March 1993.

6   Carole Giambalvo, March 1993: Information gathered during family intervention based on an assessment of Re-evaluation Counselling. See Robert J. Lifton, *Thought Reform: The Psychology of Totalism*, W. W. Norton, New York, 1961.

7   *Revelation of the Truth*, Spectrum Publications, Richmond, Victoria, for The Centre of Knowledge and Supremacy, Nunawading, Victoria, 1986.

8   Erica Heftman, on WCCO–TV, Minneapolis, Minnesota, 1980.

9   Bhagwan Rajneesh, *Sunnyas* No. 6, 1979. p. 11 in *O is for Orange . . . An examination of the Rajneesh religion, also known as the Orange People*' W. A. van Leen (ed.), Concerned Christians Growth Ministries Inc., Perth WA.

10 *I Have Come for the Sake of all Beings; An Introduction to Adi Da (the Da Avatar) and His Wisdom-Teaching*, The Dawn Horse Press for The Free Daist Avataric Communion, California USA 1995.

11 Adapted from Paul R. Martin, *Cult-Proofing Your Kids*, Zondervan, Michigan, 1993.

CHAPTER 3

1   Ronald M. Enroth, *Churches That Abuse*, Zondervan, Michigan, 1992.

2   Margaret Singer, with Janja Lalich, Jossey-Boss, San Francisco, 1996.

3   L. Booth, *When God Becomes a Drug: Breaking the Chains of Religious Addiction and Abuse*, Putnam Publishing Group, New York, 1992.

4   Singer, *op. cit.*

5   Flavil R. Yeakley, *The Disciplining Dilemma*, Gospel Advocate Press, Nashville, Tennessee, 1982, as cited in Steve Hassan, *Combatting Mind Control*, Park Street Press, Rochester, VT, 1990.

CHAPTER 4

[1] From a letter written by a cult member to Gilli Kroy's daughter, Talli.

[2] *Page One*, Channel 10, Australia.

[3] Ian Mackay, in *The Herald*, Friday, 6 July 1990.

CHAPTER 5

[1] Mary Garden, *The Serpent Rising, A Journey of Spiritual Seduction*, Brolga Publishing, Australia, 1988.

[2] Herbert L. Rosedale and Michael D. Langone, *'How Many Jonestowns Will It Take?'*, Vol. 10, No. 4, 1993, American Family Foundation, Bonita Springs, USA.

[3] C. Edwards, *Crazy for God: The Nightmare of Cult Life*, Prentice-Hall, Englewood Cliffs, NJ, 1979.

PART 2
INTRODUCTION

[1] Raphael Aron, 'Past Lives and Repressed Memories in Cults', *The Gateway Newsletter*, March 1997.

CHAPTER 6

[1] David Elias, 'Sect used drugs to recall past lives: ex-member', *The Age*, 23 September, 1994.

[2] People Forever of Australia (brochure), *Physical Immortality — the Sydney Event*, 12–13 November 1994.

[3] Robert Enroth, *The Lure of the Cults*, Intervarsity Press, Dawners Group, Ill., 1987.

[4] Louise Samways, *Dangerous Persuaders*, Penguin Books, Melbourne, 1994.

[5] Raphael Aron, 'Cults and Politics', *The Gateway Newsletter*, March 1997.

CHAPTER 7

[1] Peter Corney and Kevin Giles, *Exclusivism and The Gospel*, St Hilary's Anglican Church, Kew, Victoria, 1997.

2   *Ibid.*

3   *The Watchtower*, Vol. 116, No. 8, 6.

4   Kristen Watts, 'Strict rules tore family apart 40 years ago', *The West Australian*, 9 June 1998.

5   Wayne Jones, 'Preacher falls from grace', *The Herald Sun*, December 1993.

6   *Ibid.*

7   Paul R. Martin, *Cult Proofing Your Kids*, Zondervan, Michigan, 1993.

8   *The Sydney Morning Herald*, August 1997.

9   Ronald M. Enroth, *Churches That Abuse*, Zondervan, Michigan, 1992.

10   Kristen Watts, 'Lifetime of faith ends in Torment', *The West Australian*, 5 June 1998.

CHAPTER 8

1   *North and South*, Auckland, New Zealand, March 1993.

2   Kristen Watts, 'Ex-member: I caused splits', *The West Australian*, 13 June 1998.

3   *Ibid.* 13 June 1998.

4   Frances Adauk, 'Cult of no personality', *The Bulletin*, 26 January–26 February 1993.

5   *North and South*, Auckland, New Zealand, March 1993.

6   Grace Meertens, 'Brethren deny strict rules', *The West Australian*, 8 June 1998.

CHAPTER 9

1   A letter from Lynette Phillips some six weeks before her death in October 1978.

2   *The Sun, Wednesday Extra*, 25 July 1979.

3   *The Age*, 7 October 1978.

4   *The Sun, loc. cit.*

5   *Monday Conference*, ABC–TV, December 1978.

6   *The Daily Mail*, London, 4 October 1978.

7   Garry Barker, 'Suicide, And Our Sect: For the first time talking in the HQ of Ananda Marga', *The Herald*, 7 October 1978.

CHAPTER 10

1   Steven Kent, 'Management Training Damages Employees', *The Cult Observer*, American Family Foundation, Vol. 13, No. 2, March/April 1997.

2   ABC *Four Corners*, October 1993; *A Current Affair*, Channel 9, April 1993; *The Daily Telegraph*, 9 April 1996.

CHAPTER 11

1   'The Future Business: it saw 'em coming', *The Sunday Age*, 24 August 1997

2   Teresa Ramirez Boulette and Susan M. Anderson, 'Mind Control and the Battering of Women', *Community Mental Health Journal*, Summer 1985, Vol. 21, No. 2.

3   Louise Samways, *op. cit.*

4   Letter to Joanna from her mother, Feburary 1996.

CHAPTER 12

1   Brian Lane, *Killer Cults*, Headline Book Publishing, London, 1997.

2   *The Cult Observer*, American Family Foundation, Bonita Springs, USA, October 1985, p.8.

3   Paula Kennedy, 'Sympathy for the devil', *SHE*, April 1993.

4   Bob Tucker, 'Teen Satanism', in Michael Langone, *op. cit.*

5   Larry Kahaner, *Cults That Kill: Probing the underworld of occult crime*, Warner Books, New York, 1998.

CHAPTER 13

1   *Revelation of the Truth, op. cit.*

2   *The Herald Sun*, 5 July 1997.

3   Richard Layaco; 'The Lure of the Cults', *Time*, 7 April 1997.

4   Elizabeth Gleick, 'The Marker We've Been Waiting for', *Time*, April 1997.

5   *Virginia-Pilot and Ledger Star*, Knight-Ridder News Service, Norfolk, 1 January 1990, quoted in *AFF*, January–February 1990, p. 11.

6   *Delaware County Times*, 27 August 1989, quoted in *op. cit.*, p. 12.

7   William T. Slattery, 'Cult Was Fixated on Prophesies of Doom and

Disaster', *New York Post*, 20 April 1993 quoted in *AFF*, Vol. 10, No. 4, 1993, p. 7.

8   Leon Festinger, Henry W. Reicken, Stanley Schacter, *When Prophecy Fails*, Harper & Row, 1964.

9   Singer and Lalich, *Cults in Our Midst.*

10 *Ibid.*

Part 3
Introduction

1   Raphael Aron, 'The Dilemma of Governments', *The Gateway Newsletter*, September 1998.

Chapter 14

1   Steven Pressman, *Dangerous Betrayal, The Dark Journey of Werner Erhard from est to Exile*, Bookman Press, Australia, 1993.

2   Sarah Hamilton-Byrne, *op. cit.*

3   Jane Cafarella, 'Steiner Kinder Is Closed in Cult Row, Parents Say', *The Age*, 17 November 1994.

4   'Sect's Meeting Draws Criticism', *The Gazette*, Montreal, February 1995.

5   *The Fort Wayne (Indiana) News-Sentinel*, in M. Langone, *op. cit.*

6   Shirley Landa, 'Child Abuse in Cults', paper presented at the International Congress on Child Abuse and Neglect, Montreal, Canada, September 1984.

7   A. Markowitz. and D. A. Halperin, 'Cults and Children: The Abuse of the Young', *Cultic Studies Journal*, 1984, pp. 143–55.

8   A survivor of the Anne Hamilton-Byrne religious sect, 'We Were Screaming for Help', *Woman's Day*, February 1994.

9   Sarah Hamilton-Byrne, *op. cit.*

10 *The Age*, 23 September 1983.

11 Sarah Hamilton-Byrne, *op. cit.*

12 *Ibid.*

13 *Ibid.*

CHAPTER 15

1 From the author's counselling centre files; name changed.
2 *The Cult Observer*, American Family Foundation, July/August 1996.
3 Peter Wallsten and Diane Rado, 'Bill seeks to strip authority from HRS', *St Petersburg Times*, 4 April 1996.

PART 4
INTRODUCTION

1 'Responding to the Reality — From Deprogramming to Exit Counselling', *The Gateway Newsletter*, December 1997.

CHAPTER 16

1 Festinger, Reiken and Stanley Schacter, *op. cit.*
2 Hassan, *op. cit.*
3 *Ibid.*
4 *Ibid.*
5 *Ibid.*
6 Langone, *op. cit.*
7 L. J. West, presentation at the American Family Foundation Conference, Arlington, VA, May 1992.
8 Lifton, *op. cit.*
9 Edgar Schein, *Coercive Persuasion*, The Massachusetts Institute of Technology, W. W. Norton, San Francisco, CA, 1971.
10 Kurt Lewin, *Frontiers in Group Dynamics: Concept, Method and Reality in Social Science*, Human Relations, 1947.
11 Geri-Ann Galanti, 'Reflections on "Brainwashing"', in Michael Langone, *op. cit.*
12 Louise Samways, *op. cit.*; Steve Hassan, *op. cit.*

CHAPTER 17

1 Carol Giambalvo, *Exit Counselling, A Family Intervention*, American Family Foundation, Bonita Springs, USA, 1992. Intro. by M. Langone.
2 S. Hassan, *op. cit.*

PART 5
CHAPTER 20

[1]   *The Age*, 20 May 1992.

CHAPTER 21

[1]   'I lost my daughter to a cult' Sarah Merinos, *Family Circle*, January 1999.
[2]   E. Barker, *The Making of a Moonie*, Basil Blackwell, New York, 1984.

CHAPTER 22

[1]   Wendy Ford, *Recovery From Abusive Cults*, American Family Foundation, Bonita Springs, USA, 1990.
[2]   Raphael Aron, 'The Role of the Exit Counsellor in Reversing Mind Control', *The Gateway Newsletter*, March 1998.

PART 7
CHAPTER 26

[1]   Wendy Ford, *op. cit.*
[2]   Singer and Lalich, *op. cit.*
[3]   Steven J. Lyn and Judith Wilson (eds), *Dissociation: Clinical and Theoretical Perspectives*, Guilford Publications, New York, 1994.
[4]   Madeleine Landau Tobias, 'Guidelines for Ex-Members', in Langone, *op. cit.*

CHAPTER 27

[1]   Sarah Hamilton-Byrne, *op. cit.*
[2]   M. L. Tobias, *op. cit.*

CHAPTER 28

[1]   W. Ford, *op. cit.*

CHAPTER 29

[1]   W. Ford, *op. cit.*
[2]   Singer and Lalich, *op. cit.*

CHAPTER 30

[1] Sarah Hamilton-Byrne, *op. cit.*

[2] P. Martin, M. Langone, A. Dole and J. Wiltrout, 'Post-Cult Symptoms as Measured by the MCMI before and after Residential Treatment', *Cultic Studies Journal*, Vol. 9, No. 2, 1992, pp. 219–50.

CHAPTER 31

[1] W. Ford, *op. cit.*

[2] Arnold Markowitz, 'Guidelines for Families', in M. Langone, *op. cit.*

[3] W. Ford, *op. cit.*

[4] *Ibid.*

PART 8
CHAPTER 32

[1] Sarah Hamilton-Byrne, *op. cit.*

CHAPTER 33

[1] P. Martin, *op. cit.*

[2] C. Giambalvo, *op. cit.*

CHAPTER 34

[1] Report by an official committee of federal, state and territory governments on the issue of the criminality of cult activity. Reported in *The Australian*, 14 October 1998.

[2] Re K (1994) FLC92–461. In suggesting these guidelines, the Family Court said that they were simply guidelines; they were not rigid rules of law and a departure from them would not vitiate a judgment, although Judges, Judicial Registrars and Registrars should give sufficient reasons for so doing when they considered a departure appropriate.

[3] *North and South*, Auckland, New Zealand, March 1993.

[4] *The Australian*, October 14 1998.

[5] *Ibid.*

EPILOGUE

[1]   Section 116 of the Australian Consititution provides

> (T)he Commonwealth shall not make any law for establishing any
> religion, or for imposing any religious observance, or for prohibiting
> the free exercise of any religion, and no religious test shall be required
> as a qualification for any office or public trust under the
> Commonwealth.

*S.116 is modelled on s.3 of Article VI and the First Amendment to
the United States Constitution.*

For a full discussion, see *Free to Believe? The Right to Freedom of Religion
and Belief in Australia,* Human Rights Commissioner Discussion Paper
No. 1, February 1997, Human Rights and Equal Opportunity
Commission, Sydney 1997.

[2]   Gary D. Bouma, *People and Place,* Vol.5, No.3, p. 112.

[3]   Jeannie Mills, defector from Jim Jones' People's Temple, who was
subsequently murdered. Paul R. Martin, *Cult-proofing Your Kids,*
Zondervan, Michigan, 1993.

Bibliography

Ankerberg, J. & Weldon, J., *Cult Watch: What You Need to Know About Spiritual Deception*, Harvest House Publishers, Oregon, 1991

Arterburn, Stephen & Felton Jack, *Toxic Faith, Understanding and Overcoming Religious Addiction*, Thomas Nelson, Nashville, 1991

Atack, Jon, *A Piece of Blue Sky — Scientology, Dianetics and L.Ron Hubbard Exposed*, Carol Publishing Group, New York, 1990

Barker, E., *The Making of a Moonie*, Basil Blackwell, New York, 1984

Barron, Bruce, *If You Really Want to Follow Jesus*, Partners Press, Sycamore IL, 1981

Boettcher, Robert, *Gifts of Deceit – Sun Myong Moon, Tongsun Park and the Korean Scandal*, Holt Rinehart and Winston, New York, 1980

Booth, Leo, *When God Becomes a Drug, Breaking the Chains of Religious Addiction and Abuse*, Putnam Publishing Group, New York, 1992

Brasswell G.W., *Understanding Sectarian Groups in America*, Broadman, Nashville, 1986

Brooke, Tal, *Riders of the Cosmic Circuit: Rajneesh, Sai Baba, Muktananda. . . Gods of the New Age*, Lion, Batavia, IL, 1986

Conway and Siegelman, *Snapping: America's Epidemic of Sudden Personality Change*, Second Edition , Stillpoint Press, New York, 1995,

Corney, Peter and Giles, Kevin, *Exclusivism and the Gospel*, St Hilary's Anglican Church, Kew, Victoria, 1997

Davis, Deborah Berg, *The Children of God: The Inside Story*, Zondervan, Grand Rapids, Michigan, 1984

Dellinger, R., *Cults and Kids: A Study of Coercion*, Boys Town, Nebraska, 1985

Edwards, C., *Crazy for God, The Nightmare of Cult Life*, Prentice-Hall, Englewood Cliffs, New Jersey, 1979

Eisenberg, Gary D., *Smashing the Idols: A Jewish Enquiry into the Cult Phenomenon*, Jason Aronson, Northvale, New Jersey, 1988

Enroth, Ronald M., *Churches That Abuse*, Zondervan, Michigan, 1992

Festinger, Leon; Reicken H.W. & Schacter, Stanley, *When Prophecy Fails: A Social and Psychological Study of a Modern Group that Predicted the Destruction of the World*, Harper & Row, New York, 1964

Ford, Wendy, *Recovery from Abusive Cults*, The American Family Foundation, Bonita Springs, Florida,1990

Garden, Mary, *The Serpent Rising, A Journey of Spiritual Seduction*, Brolga Publishing, Queensland, 1988

Giambalvo, Carol, *Exit Counselling: A Family Intervention*, The American Family Foundation, Bonita Springs, Florida, 1992

Gordon, James S., *The Golden Guru*, The Stephen Greene Press, Lexington, MA,1987

Gore, Tipper, *Raising PG Kids in an X-Rated Society*, Abingdon Press, Nashville, 1987

Hamilton-Byrne, Sarah, *Unseen, Unheard, Unknown*, Penguin Books, Melbourne, 1995

Hassan, Steven, *Combatting Cult Mind Control*, Park Street Press, Rochester, Vermont, 1988

Hearst, Patricia Campbell with Moscow, Alvin, *Every Secret Thing*, Pinnacle, New York, 1982

Heftmann, Erica, *Dark Side of the Moonies*, Penguin, Sydney,1982

Hubner, J. and Gruson, L., *Monkey on a Stick: Murder, Madness and the Hari Krishnas*, Harcourt, Brace and Jovanovich, 1988

Johnson, David and VanVonderen, Jeff, *The Subtle Power of Spiritual Abuse*, Bethany House, Minneapolis, 1991

Jones, Jerry, *What Does the Boston Movement Teach?* Mid-America Book and Tape Sales, Bridgeton MO, 1990

Kahaner, Larry, *Cults that Kill: Probing the Underworld of Occult Crime*, Warner Books, New York, 1988

Kilduff, M. and Javers, R., *The Suicide Cult: The Inside Story of the People's Temple Sect and the Massacre in Guyana*, Bantam, New York, 1978

King, Dennis, *Lyndon LaRouche and the New American Fascism*, Double Day, New York, 1989

Lane, Brian, *Killer Cults*, Headline Book Publishing, London, 1997

Langone, Michael D., Blood, Linda O, *Satanism and Occult-Related Violence: What You Should Know,* American Family Foundation, Weston, MA., 1990

Larson, Bob, *Satanism, the Seduction of America's Youth,* Thomas Nelson, Nashville, 1989

Lifton, Robert Jay, *Thought Reform and the Psychology of Totalism,* W.W Norton, New York, 1961

Lyn, S.J., and Wilson, J., *Dissociation: Clinical and Theoretical Perspectives,* Guilford Publications, New York, 1994

Penton, James, *Apocalypse Delayed: The Story of Jehovah's Witnesses,* University of Toronto Press, Toronto, 1985

Persinger, M.A et al., *TM and Cult Mania,* The Chistopher Publishing House, North Quincy, MA 1980

Martin, W. and Klann, N. *Jehovah of the Watchtower,* Bethany House, Minneapolis, 1981

Martin, Paul R., *Cult-Proofing Your Kids,* Zondervan, Michigan, 1993

Maury T., *The Ultimate Evil,* Doubleday, New York, 1987

Milne, Hugh, *Bhagwan: The God That Failed,* St Martin's Press, New York, 1987

Pressman, Steven, *Dangerous Betrayal, The Dark Journey of Werner Erhard from Est to Exile,* Bookman Press, Melbourne, 1993

Rhinehart, L., *The Book of Est,* Hilt, Rinehart and Winston, New York, 1976

Rosen, R.D, *Psychobabble,* Atheneum, New York, 1977

Rudin, James and Rudin, Marcia, *Prison or Paradise? The New Religious Cults,* Fortress Press, Philadelphia, 1980

Rutter, Peter, *Sex in the Forbidden Zone,* Jeremy P. Tarcher Inc., Los Angeles, 1989

Samways, Louise, *Dangerous Persuaders,* Penguin Books, Melbourne 1994

Schein, E.H. with Schneier, I & Barker, C.H., *Coercive Persuasion: A Socio-psychological Analysis of the "Brainwashing" of American Civilian Prisoners by the Chinese Communists,* W.W. Norton, New York 1961

Singer, Margaret with Lalich Janja, *Cults in Our Midst,* Jossey-Boss, San Francisco 1996

Sprecher, P, 'The Cult as a Total Institution: Perceptual Distortion, Consensual Validation and Independent Decision Making' delivered to the panel 'Taking the Cults to Court', Conference on Law and Society, Washington D.C., June 1987

Strelley, Kate, *The Ultimate Game: The Rise and Fall of Bhagwan Shree Rajneesh,* Harper & Row, New York 1987

Tanner, Jerald and Sandra, *The Changing World f Mormonism,* Moody Press, Chicago, 1981

Tobias, M.L. and Lalich J., *Captive Hearts, Captive Minds: Freedom and Recovery from Cults and Abusive Relationships,* Hunter House, Alameda, California, 1994

Vicky, J., *Sex in the Sect,* Essien, Melbourne 1995

Watson, William, *A Concise Dictionary of Cults and Religions,* Moody Press, Chicago, 1991

Zaretsky, Irving I, Leone, Mark P., *Religious Movements in Contemporary America,* Princeton University Press, New Jersey, 1974